THE LIGHT OF
HIS FACE

Spirituality for Catholic Teachers

John Bollan

VERITAS

For Frank and Josephine Bollan

Optimis parentibus

First published 2007 by
Veritas Publications
7/8 Lower Abbey Street
Dublin 1
Ireland
Email publications@veritas.ie
Website www.veritas.ie

ISBN 978 1 84730 022 5

A catalogue record for this book
is available from the British Library.

Printed in the Republic of Ireland
by Betaprint Dublin

Veritas books are printed on paper made from the wood pulp of managed forests. For every tree felled, at least one tree is planted, thereby renewing natural resources.

CONTENTS

'What can bring us happiness?' many say.
Lift up the light of your face on us, O Lord.
(Psalm 4)

ACKNOWLEDGEMENTS

Singling out those individuals who have contributed to the production of this book is an invidious task: I hope none of my 'significant others' will be offended if, by an oversight, I forget to mention them.

I would like to thank my colleagues in Religious Education at Glasgow University, especially Dr Bob Davis, Head of Department, and Professor James Conroy, Dean of the Faculty. Everyone in the Department is a source of encouragement and inspiration, although a special word of thanks goes to Liz Brown, Denise Bula and Sharon Cumming for their aesthetic judgements. Michael McGrath, Director of the Scottish Catholic Education Service and part of our extended departmental family, has also been most supportive – not least in graciously consenting to contribute the Foreword.

Bishop John Mone, Bishop Emeritus of Paisley, has truly been a father to me (and all his priests) and I send my thanks to him and his successor, Bishop Philip Tartaglia. I also owe a debt of sincere gratitude to those priests who have taught me so much simply by their charity and good humour in putting up with me: Monsignor Gerry Brennan, Monsignor Willie Diamond and Father Brian McGee. With them I thank the good people of Saint Joseph's, Clarkston, Saint Margaret's, Johnstone, and Saint Mirin's Cathedral, Paisley. Thanks also to Father John Keenan, the well-respected Roman Catholic Chaplain at the University of Glasgow who was the inspiration behind the reflection on page 80. Among the many other priests who also deserve my thanks is Father Eamonn Mulcahy CSSp: I hope he will receive this book as a token of esteem and affection.

I thank all those teachers who have given me a wealth of positive experiences and a love of teaching. My students have also taught me a great deal and it would be remiss not to acknowledge their influence on me and what you will read in these pages.

Christopher Morris was generous with his time and help with the original typescript. Thereafter Niamh McGarry, Donna Doherty and Ruth Garvey at Veritas steered the project through to completion.

Finally, although this book is already dedicated to them, I would like to express my heartfelt gratitude to my parents, Frank and Josephine. Their love, on both sides of eternity, sustains our family each day. I am sure that it is their example which has made my sisters Evelyn and Helen so loving and offers me some hope, some day, of being like them.

John Bollan

FOREWORD

John Bollan's publication of *The Light of His Face* is most timely. Catholic teachers, working in various contexts to deliver Catholic education today, face significant challenges. In addition to the demands on them to deliver learning and teaching of the highest quality, they are also expected to lead children and young people in the search for truth. Meanwhile, significant forces in society are challenging the very notion of truth and the place of religious faith and values in society.

This book offers hope and encouragement to teachers who are seeking to continue their personal formation in faith and to ground their spirituality in Jesus Christ. Using non-theological language, Fr Bollan gently but firmly leads readers towards deep insights into Christian faith and the Catholic tradition. Throughout this journey, he never forgets that he is forming teachers whose focus will always be on how they can use their own knowledge and understanding to support their students. This book is grounded in practicality as well as spirituality.

Many Church documents since Vatican II have offered guidance on the Church's expectations of teachers who are engaged in Catholic education. One of these describes teachers as 'teachers of learning and of life [who] may be a reflection, albeit imperfect but still vivid, of the One Teacher'.[1] I am certain that *The Light of His Face* will help

---

1   *The Catholic School on the Threshold of the Third Millennium,* 1998.

teachers, in all their imperfections and vulnerabilities, to realise how they can reflect the light of Jesus the Teacher, even in a world which appears to be ever darkening.

Michael McGrath
Director, Scottish Catholic Education Service
February 2007

INTRODUCTION

In one of those typically resonant phrases of his, Pope John Paul II wrote that 'the future of humanity passes by way of the family' (*Familiaris consortio*, 86). Few would argue with this. It is no exaggeration to suggest that humanity is indeed shaped by the kind of relationships we experience in these cradles of society. Yet what is true of the family also holds true for the environment in which we spend so much of our formative years – the school. This is even truer of the relationship between the Catholic Church and the schools that spring from its rich tradition of faith and learning. The book in your hands is born of the conviction that, to a great extent, *the future of the Church passes by way of its schools.* For an increasing number of children and young people in our society, the context of faith formation has shifted away from the family and the parish community to the school. While this may not be the ideal, it is pretty much the reality.

And so the mantle of catechist is being placed on young and, in some cases, uncertain shoulders; some of those entering the teaching profession are themselves part of a generation whose contact with faith has been grounded in the classroom rather than the home or the Church. How do we support their development so that they are just as confident in their identity as Catholic educators as they are in their roles as teachers of language or science?

That is precisely the challenge before us at the University of Glasgow where we are charged with the formation of large numbers of young teachers desiring to pursue their careers in Catholic schools. By the same token, the wider Catholic community looks to us to support the ongoing development of our teachers in the sometimes fraught interface between a faith commitment and a demanding professional life in an increasingly secular environment. The concepts and ideas in this book are drawn from the programme of *Catholic Teacher Formation* running across the Faculty of Education. This volume is not meant to be a study of catechetics or the theology of pedagogy; I try to avoid using language that is overtly technical or academic and, when I do, it is simply because it fits best. It is hoped that some of the thoughts presented here, rooted as they are in pastoral life and classroom experience, may be of help to anyone who has an interest in the spiritual dimension of teaching from beginning teachers through to highly experienced practitioners. While these reflections are robustly Catholic, I hope that fellow travellers from other faith traditions may also find something that strikes a chord with their own situation.

This book is in two parts. The first part offers a series of reflections on the ways in which teaching has clear spiritual overtones. Some passages from scripture are considered from a classroom perspective in the hope that teachers might find they have much in common with the experiences of Jesus and his disciples. The second part of the book offers a practical tool-kit of materials to assist students and teachers in developing their own faith formation programme.

These reflections begin and end with reference to two distinct but related icons: the icons of the Transfigured Christ and of Divine Love Enfleshed, better known as the Sacred Heart of Jesus. Everything in these pages bears the imprint of those iconic depictions of Christ. They are sources of inspiration, love, wonder, *light*. Light is one of the key elements in the accounts of those encounters with Jesus. The faltering human expressions of what it was like to meet Christ are suffused with light. That, then, must surely be the starting point and goal of any faith journey: *to walk by the light of his face* and find ourselves transformed in the process.

John Bollan
University of Glasgow

PART I

REFLECTIONS FROM SCRIPTURE AND THE CLASSROOM

A WORD ABOUT SPIRITUALITY

Blowing in the wind

Today many people are more comfortable describing themselves as 'spiritual' than 'religious'. I suppose in our increasingly secular and materialistic world we should be grateful even for that. To my mind, the best visual expression of this is a scene in the film *American Beauty*. Although some might raise their eyebrows at a movie which takes a subversive approach to domestic propriety, it is actually quite a moral story. It shows us two young loners who drift together, finding common cause in their contempt for the perceived hypocrisies of their parents' generation and its stifling routines. One day the boy shows the girl a film of the most beautiful thing he has ever seen. While we might expect footage of a sunset or a mountain panorama, what he gives us is a silent movie of a white grocery bag blown about by the wind. The word he uses to describe its motion is *dancing*. This discarded bit of plastic is dancing with him and in doing so it makes him aware of an unseen force behind things, a reassuring and consoling presence. Those teenagers speak for a whole generation – indeed more than one generation – who want to rebel against the suffocation of their spirits. We have a hard-wired sensitivity to what the boy calls 'this incredibly benevolent force' and in describing themselves as spiritual most people are implicitly affirming this. What sets the twenty-first century apart is the way most of us are happy to leave that force without a name and our relationship with it free of the constraints of words and images. *It just is.*

Since this a book about spirituality and the spiritual lives of educators, it might be worthwhile clarifying what is meant by this increasingly vague word. To borrow the imagery of the film for a little longer, we are indeed moved and guided by this force. We experience its energy, *impelled* and *propelled* throughout our lives. Beyond the apparent randomness and occasional solitude of our existence, there is the intimacy and rhythm of something very like a dance. This is God moving with us, through us, in us. Spirituality is, first and foremost, the awareness of this energy we call grace. It is grace which takes us as it finds us and moves us closer to God. Or rather, since God is everywhere, it simply makes us more conscious of that loving presence. Spirituality also describes the *ways* and the *language* in which we express our relationship with God and our fellow seekers-after-God. Although we respond to God in ways which are uniquely personal, we do not do so in isolation. We are enriched by the insight and experience of those who have surrendered to the motions of grace. By reflecting on their accounts of darkness and light, agony and ecstasy, we get a sense of our bearings. For Christians there is a treasury of accumulated wisdom stretching back thousands of years to the pages of the Old Testament. In Jesus we have someone to get to grips with in making sense of our spiritual lives. He reveals this force as 'Father' and this wind as 'Spirit':

> The wind blows wherever it pleases. You hear its sound, but you cannot tell where it comes from or where it is going. So it is with everyone born of the Spirit. (John 3:8)

We are not blowing aimlessly through life. No matter how absurd and circuitous our route may seem, grace moves us in the right path. The Holy Spirit knows where it is going. This same Spirit breathes through the diaries and stories of the

Saints in which their own spiritualities are preserved or, better still, alive and accessible to us. In this book there are echoes of Ignatius, Benedict, Augustine, Margaret Mary and many others. While their writings are sometimes regarded as brands or schools of spirituality, they are all expressions of a desire to live ever more fully the life of Christ. As teachers we certainly have something to learn from them. At the same time, *we* are also moved by grace and we should be attentive to what the Spirit is saying to us. Do not be afraid to sketch out *your* spiritual vision because that is something Christ is doing in you. At least that is the way I understand those final words in John's Gospel about the whole world being too small a place to contain all the books about Christ. We are all still writing.

'TELL AND SHOW'

The Transfiguration as Learning Environment

As soon as I had typed the above sentence I was overcome with a strong urge to change it. Anyone glancing at the words 'The Transfiguration as Learning Environment' might well be tempted to shut the book as quickly as possible for fear of being buried under an avalanche of edu-babble. That said, I decided to keep the title as it is, for the simple reason that the terminology of the classroom should not be kept separate from the language of faith: grace can seep into the cracks and wrinkles of human experience and education is no exception.

In this chapter I would like to explore the Transfiguration of Jesus, both as it is recounted in the Gospel and depicted in sacred art. Cardinal Carlo Maria Martini penned a brilliant pastoral letter on this very subject which has been translated as *Saving Beauty*. I recommend it to anyone who wants to approach this key episode from an aesthetic angle. My main aim in this reflection is to consider the Transfiguration as a 'lesson' prepared by Christ. Just how 'successful' the lesson was, is for you to evaluate.

Background to the lesson

It is important for us to consider the disciples as learners. The very word 'disciple' implies a relationship of listening and learning. Jesus very clearly assumes the role of 'Rabbi' or teacher and the Gospels are quite unambiguous in describing much of his activity as 'teaching'. Even those 'bits' of his ministry which do not involve instruction, such as healings or exorcisms, are meant to convey a clear message about the nearness of God's Kingdom. The real thrust of his mission is the culmination of what we call the Paschal Mystery, the events surrounding his suffering, death and resurrection.

This is the background for the 'lesson' of the Transfiguration. Ever since the rather embarrassing end to John the Baptist's ministry, Jesus is increasingly focused on his own. The full horror of the impending crucifixion is hard for us to grasp, accustomed as we are to the happy ending of the story. For the disciples, however, the idea that their friend and teacher could be exposed to the most accursed of deaths was so extreme as to be inconceivable. So the events on the mountain are designed to help the disciples, especially the privileged inner circle of Peter, James and John, to jump the gap between the abject awfulness of the cross and the hidden workings of providence.

The lesson itself

The Gospels all agree that the Transfiguration takes place on a high mountain, with Mark and Matthew adding a note of privacy: although this is to be an *elevated* experience, there is also an element of *intimacy* to the gathering. Perhaps to this note of privacy should be added a hint of individuality. Although the disciples are there as a little group, Jesus intends each one of them to take something unique from the encounter. The physical location of the Transfiguration is important not just in providing a *setting* (the higher we go, the more our perspectives are altered) but also for the *effort* which is required to get there. Luke adds a little detail which is also significant: the ostensible purpose of their hike is to pray and it is against the backdrop of prayer that the transformation occurs.

Suddenly, without warning, Jesus changes. While all three evangelists comment on the brilliance of Christ's clothing, Luke and Matthew note a change in his aspect: 'his face shone like the sun' (Matthew 17:2). The light comes from within him, like the sun. This transformation is not brought out about by any outside agency. Jesus is not 'floodlit on Tabor'. Then the next element of the lesson unfolds: Moses and Elijah appear on either side of Jesus and speak with him (although only Luke ventures to suggest what their conversation was about). It is traditionally considered that these figures represent the two great streams of religious inspiration – law and prophecy. Jesus appears firmly within the context of his people's religious understanding and yet adds something *new*. 'His passing which he was to accomplish in Jerusalem' (Luke 9:31) is hinted at in the foregoing 'lessons' of the law and the prophetic utterances of Israel but this next step is a radical and challenging one. His passing is going to be accomplished through rejection, suffering and death. Christ is leading his disciples to an awareness of what his words about the cross *actually mean* for them all; not some metaphorical surrender of life but a nasty and brutal seizing of it.

What is really happening in this privileged moment? The disciples are offered, albeit for a fleeting instant, a chance to see Jesus as his Father sees him. This is a moment of true insight. Peter, James and John are *seeing in* to Christ through the eyes of Love itself. Love, which has the power to transform the 'ordinariness' of life, allows the disciples to bask in the light of a radiance which is in Jesus all the time. Not all insights can be clearly articulated. Peter clutches at words to convey something of the depth of their wonder (only Mark refers to it as fear). It is easy to be patronising about his suggestion to pitch tents; no matter how daft it may sound, Peter is trying to get hold of this event and break it up into manageable concepts. He is taking a transcendent experience and trying to fit it into the framework of his understanding of the world and its workings. This is not to be scoffed at: Peter is attempting what any intelligent person would do.

To use the language of lesson planning, what Jesus intends the disciples to take from the experience is an image of himself in glory, reinforced by the words of the Father that he is 'the Beloved'. The next time they see Jesus in a similar setting it will be under very changed circumstances: not in glory, but utter humiliation; not in the company of God's spokesmen, but of two condemned criminals – and his fate no better than theirs. Although this is the intended outcome of this particular episode, it would be fair to say that the disciples are on a fairly steep learning curve and do not immediately grasp what Jesus has been trying to get across. They fail to understand what 'rising from the dead' could mean (nor do they ask the teacher!) and allow the sorrowful spectacle of Golgotha to drive the lesson of Tabor from their minds. It is only much further down the road that these three disciples are able to reflect back on their experience and the connection is successfully made.

Looking at Christ: 'Eye contact' for the teacher

The Transfiguration is chiefly a visual experience: the 'lesson' is conveyed by looking at Jesus, rather than simply attending to the voice of the Father. Virtually all the artistic imaginings of this Gospel episode show the disciples shielding their eyes against the glare of glory. This seems to be something of a missed opportunity, especially as Luke suggests that they 'stayed awake' to miss nothing of this awesome spectacle. Teachers are only too aware of the value of illustration: a well-used image can be twice as effective as words. But the purpose of their looking at Christ is also bound up with the way in which he had looked at them – indeed, *into* them. The lofty mountain setting serves to underscore the 'leg up' that this Transfiguration is giving the disciples in terms of their perspective. Not only are they seeing Jesus as the Father sees him; they are also seeing *themselves* as Jesus sees them. Their potential for goodness and greatness is unlocked by Christ's insight. He has the gift to 'look and love' and see what is lacking in someone's life; his penetrating but respectful gaze provokes the amazed response 'but how do you know me?'.

Eye contact often features in the arsenal of classroom management: a quelling look can put down a potential mutiny. I have seen teachers who would have made Genghis Khan turn-tail with a raised eyebrow. Yet by far the most important element of eye contact is the tacit signal it sends: 'I see you.' Some of the most self-destructive behaviours in life often issue from a sense of futility; that nothing matters, that nothing I do (good or bad) gets noticed. To counter this Jesus says quite clearly that the Father sees all that is done in secret. This loving scrutiny is not some invasion of privacy: we are God's business. 'Why, every hair on your head has been counted.' The Transfiguration invites teachers to make eye contact with Christ and to see themselves reflected in that light. Teachers, in turn, are called to look at others in the same way, especially those poorest of children who are starved of love and frequently ignored. In other words, these rough-edged 'weans' (children) have never been *looked into shape* by someone who genuinely respects and cares for them. To 'look someone into shape' is to make them aware that they are seen, understood and accepted. Even if not everything they do can be *approved of*, they are still *accepted*. Disruptive behaviour may be a form of attention seeking, but there are times when it is simply a by-product of feeling insignificant. It does not matter what you do because you do not matter either.

What I am trying to say might be better served by an illustration. One of the most moving aspects of the story of Lourdes is the way Bernadette describes the eye contact she made with 'the Lady' in the grotto. As a young girl, especially with her poor, unlettered background, Bernadette would frequently be addressed in the curtest of terms. Seldom would anyone take the trouble to actually *look* at her while speaking to her. What struck Bernadette about the

Lady was that she looked at her 'as one person looks at another'. She was left in no doubt that she was the object of the vision's attention and words requesting – *politely* – that Bernadette might do her the courtesy of coming back to the grotto for two weeks. Those words are certainly full of grace, and brought about an equally gracious response: grace invites graciousness.

Beauty in a world of ugliness

The Transfiguration affirms beauty, especially that extraordinary beauty which shows itself in unexpected places. There is a real need for beauty in our world. We are constantly bombarded with images 'which some viewers might find upsetting' (as the newsreaders warn us): death, famine, disease, violence. The explosion of the Internet means that these distressing images are only ever a mouse-click away. A couple of years ago I found myself sitting at the 'Internet corner' of a hotel lobby beside a child who was browsing through autopsy photographs. When I pointed out to him that that sort of thing wasn't for children he looked at me as if *I* were a monster. I am very concerned about the potential after-effects of exposing children to such images of real-life horror. There is, I think, a kind of stealth trauma which creeps up on children (and adults) when they are subjected to a drip-feed of such images. Not that long ago I was observing a student teach a very impressive lesson to a Primary One class. She had her little charges sitting around her chair, legs in a basket, gazing up at her as she showed them some pictures of autumn. 'Now, boys and girls, I'm going to show you an amazing picture,' she told the class with infectious enthusiasm. One little boy sitting beside her chair recoiled and covered his eyes pleading, 'Miss, don't show me anything yucky!' My first reaction was to smile at this oversensitivity but then I wondered just how many yucky things he might have seen in his short life. The world is only too full of *yuckiness*.

What the Transfiguration offers is an antidote to all that conspires against beauty. The three figures on the mountain-top also mirror a triptych of Gospel scenes, with the Passion and the Resurrection completing this story arc or rainbow of theological colour. Although brutality and disfigurement dominate the central scene, these give way to the beauty which precedes and follows. The sadness of Christ's death gives way to the bright promise of immortality. It is worth remembering that this pattern is also played out in life in general. Whenever we enter the 'dark night', be it in our private or professional lives, it is important to remember that it will pass. We may be overshadowed for a time, but *only* for a time.

Tell and show: Witnesses on the ground

Matthew and Mark's accounts more or less end with Jesus instructing the apostles to say nothing about what they witnessed; Luke opts for a spontaneous 'vow of silence' on their part. At first sight this may sound slightly odd. Surely they would have been bursting to tell the others what they had seen. Why should they wait until 'after the Son of Man had risen from the dead', whatever *that* might mean? My handle on this apparent conundrum is that Jesus is using a layered teaching approach: the full impact of the experience will only become clear later. I find this to be especially true of students in teacher-formation programmes. What they are being offered by their teachers sometimes appears of dubious relevance in the short-term. You might receive positive feedback from students on an enjoyable lecture presentation but still hear niggling doubts about its practical value. Students often voice a desire simply to be taught what to teach, as if being a page ahead of the class were enough. My students have become familiar with the mantra, 'You may not get this right now, but later on you will see'! As I have suggested above, the disciples are only to grasp the depth of this encounter in the light of Easter. It is then that they can begin to witness to the whole mystery of Christ.

Although the disciples are described as witnesses we should not overlook the fact that Jesus himself is 'the faithful witness' (Revelation 1:5). His teaching is not just about *telling*, but *showing* as well. This sets out the pattern which his disciples are to follow as they extend the Gospel message to the ends of the earth. Their witness is not just a matter of words. The Word became flesh and so their words must also take solid form in their lives and actions. As much as I love Raphael's famous mosaic of the Transfiguration in Saint Peter's Basilica, I am a little disappointed that the three central figures are levitating, caught up in an eddy of wind and light. To a generation brought up on a diet of science-fiction imagery, they look like alien abductees with the spaceship just out of the frame. The icons of Eastern Christianity seem more faithful to the Gospel account: Jesus, Moses and Elijah are standing on solid ground. For all the transcendent power of this event, at no point does anyone involved lose touch with the earth.

No matter how heavenly it may be, the message of the Gospel needs to be grounded in reality. It is far too easy to take the Word made flesh and turn it back into words again. The key challenge for the Catholic teacher is to witness to the whole package of the faith and to ensure that their words are confirmed by their actions. What our children and young people need are *real people* engaged in living the faith in the often messy circumstances of the twenty-first century. Teaching reinforced by example is the authentic continuation of Christ's ministry. Here was one who taught with authority and not like the scribes. His witness was genuine and compelling because he was being true to himself.

If we as teachers are to be true to him and his 'lesson plan', we must be prepared to replicate his methods and those of the disciples. Their witness took on a new shape when they were asked to embrace suffering. This they were able to do because the light of Tabor was never fully extinguished in their hearts and minds. Even when the demands of the Gospel conflicted with the 'normal and sensible' options offered by the world – such as the chance of staying alive – they chose martyrdom, which is the most exalted form of witness there is.

The next time you stand in front of a class and find the words are dying on your lips, and your heart is overshadowed, look at your feet: they are planted on the same earth that witnessed the awesome transformation of Jesus and the inner illumination of his friends. Then look at the class: if the eyes looking back at you are filled with boredom, indifference or incomprehension, *do not despair*. This is just one moment in the unfolding of understanding which started before you and does not end with you. All that you have to give in that moment, in that place, is *yourself*. Offer that, and the circuit between you and that high mountain-top will be complete. The class may not be dazzled, but you should become more aware of your own light. You might even catch your inner voice echoing those words of Peter, 'It is wonderful for us to be here'.

Reflection

An interesting aspect of Raphael's Transfiguration *is that he brings his visual account of Christ in glory together with the next episode in the Gospel. The 'top tier' of the painting shows Christ caught up in shining splendour while, at the foot of the mountain, the boy possessed by an unclean spirit is being brought along by his anguished parents. Here it is Raphael who is offering us a lesson through art: here he shows us what such moments of clarity and insight are actually for. What we experience on the the high places is always in the service of what we are asked to do in the plain, ordinary moments of life. Notice too that the Transfiguration represents an all too brief respite from the harsh demands of Jesus' ministry.*

We should not be altogether caught out by the rapid alteration between triumph and challenge, between the sublime and the mundane.

DEEP WATER
Rediscovering Teaching as Vocation

When He asked the woman of Samaria for water
to drink,
Christ had already prepared for her the gift of
faith.
In His thirst to receive her faith
He awakened in her heart the fire of Your love.
Preface of the 2nd Sunday of Lent

I recently celebrated Mass for the fiftieth anniversary reunion
of graduates of Notre Dame College of Education in
Glasgow. Notre Dame College no longer exists, having
merged with Edinburgh's Craiglockhart College to form
Saint Andrew's College of Education. That institution,
which was Scotland's national centre for 'Catholic teacher
training' for three decades, merged in its turn with the
department of education at Glasgow University giving birth
to the Faculty in which I now teach. This proud genealogy
means that the University of Glasgow tries to provide a home
for generations of graduates from these parent institutions. It
was for this reason that I was given the honour of officiating
at the reunion and the day overflowed with memories for
everyone concerned (my *first ever* teacher and the Head
Teacher of another school where I taught were both
members of the class of 1955). The Faculty building is itself
a repository of memory: grainy photographs of Edwardian
student teachers adorn the walls of the Religious Education
room along with photographs of Pope John Paul II's visit to
Saint Andrew's College on June 1982. During that visit the
Holy Father had these words for the staff and students:

In reflecting on the value of Catholic schools and the importance of Catholic teachers and educators, it is necessary to stress the central point of Catholic education itself. Catholic education is above all a question of communicating Christ, of helping to form Christ in the lives of others. Those who have been baptised must be trained to live the newness of Christian life in justice and in the holiness of truth. The cause of Catholic education is the cause of Jesus Christ and of his Gospel at the service of man.

Although he makes reference to baptismal newness of life and the service of others, it is striking that the Pope does not use the word 'vocation' at any point in his address. Perhaps we should not read too much into this omission; his other teachings are replete with references to vocation. But this instance does echo something that happened at about the same time in educational circles: talk of vocation disappeared from educational discourse. Some may argue that 'disappeared' is too strong a word – better to say it 'slipped out' for a bit. This may have happened because *it went without saying* that Catholic education enshrines a vision of teaching as vocation. Equally, however, it might be suggested that other forces engaged in shaping educational philosophy and policy outgrew that terminology (and maybe felt a little embarrassed by it). The subtle introduction of consumerist language and the onslaught of professional initiatives tended to squeeze out the fuzzy notion of vocation. How do I know this? Well, I belong to a generation which came through that phase and the only time I heard the word 'vocation' was at the Mass for the beginning of the term. We had 'reflective practitioner' coming out of our ears but the 'v' word was conspicuous by its absence.

That reunion Mass for the class of 1955 was an unambiguous celebration of vocation. These 'girls' themselves had fond memories of those Notre Dame Sisters who had passed on their deeply held educational beliefs to them. Prominent among these was a conviction that teaching was a God-given call, bringing with it the challenges and graces of anything undertaken in the name of Christ and his Church. Some people look at the struggles of the Church today and diagnose a crisis of vocation or identity. If this is true, and to a certain extent I am prepared to accept that it is, then a sensible starting point for recovery is to rediscover this identity and reclaim the 'v' word from its fuzzy detractors.

The Scriptures are of course a rich source of vocation stories from Moses to Peter, Esther to Mary. In this chapter I would like to spend some time in the company of another woman, perhaps a less obvious choice. Indeed the fact that Jesus chose to spend *any* time in her company was a cause of some scandal to the disciples. I am referring to the Samaritan woman at the well of Sychar in Chapter 4 of John's Gospel.

What I enjoy most about this story is the way it begins with the dusty, thirsty reality of a journey under the hot sun. If you open this page of the Gospel you can almost see the heat haze. Equally refreshing is the fairly pedestrian banter which gets the scene underway. John, so fond of theology, gives us some delightful statements of the obvious: the woman points out that Jesus is a Jew (breaking news) and that he has no bucket (well spotted)! These observations serve to underscore the fact that the woman is very much operating at a superficial level. Her life is a series of monotonous to-ings and fro-ings with the well at the centre. So much of her time and energy is expended in this way that she has little left of either to probe more deeply beneath the surface of her life. But every journey needs a starting point and this is as good as any. Jesus is a bit like a travelling salesman, using the request for water as a 'foot in the door' and drawing the woman into conversation. Her initial reluctance is soon overcome and she opens up a lively dialogue with this stranger.

The discourse about Living Water which follows is a beautiful meditation on the gift of the Holy Spirit. Our friend, still taking things a bit too literally, expresses a desire for this Water to end the daily drudgery of water carrying. Bit by bit, however, Jesus leads her to realise that it is not just the well that is deep. There is a longing for something – or a thirst – that goes deep into this woman's life. As they speak (and I would like to think that Jesus has been given that drink he had asked for), layer by layer of the woman's life is peeled back. Now she begins to see just how she got there. Not in the mundane sense of every step she had taken, there and back, thousands of times in her life. This was a true moment of revelation: here was a man who told her everything she had ever done! Perhaps Jesus had helped her scrape away at the dry surface of her life until hidden springs of truth began to flow. There was no longer any need to hide the reality of her relationships from anyone – least of all herself. 'You spoke the truth there' is a wonderful statement of discovery, the heart's '*Eureka*'! The deluge of honesty and self-recognition swept away all those little compromises she had made with herself. Now it began to fall into place. A Jewish stranger had succeeded in unlocking that complex knot of questions she was carrying around inside herself about God, the world and her place in it. Her amazement chimes perfectly with the sense of wonder we hear in the psalm: 'your eyes saw all my actions, they were all of them written in your book' (Psalm 138:16).

The woman at the well experiences a reversal of the fortunes of her predecessor in Genesis Chapter 2. Instead of being drawn into a destructive dialogue, this man lets her experience God's knowing her as the most natural thing in the world. No need for her to hide among metaphorical bushes. No need to hide the truth from herself any longer. Is it any wonder she ran to tell the others?

What is significant about this encounter is the way in which past, present and future come together. The events of her life make sense in that moment and that moment, in turn, propels her into a changed future. She becomes a disciple. She becomes someone who brings others to Christ, not keeping that life-giving encounter to herself but gladly sharing it with others. That is the essence of the Christian calling and certainly the vocation of a Catholic teacher. It is a call which

- begins with Christ and develops in conversation with him
- often goes unheard and unacknowledged, buried under layers of our personal history
- persists in spite of (and sometimes *through*) the messy relationships and poor choices we enter upon
- once heard, echoes throughout our lives.

Teachers, as much as priests and religious, should engage in their own reflection on the emerging pattern of their lives. God has been involved in those lives from the beginning. As the saying goes, our stories are *his-story*. Perhaps as we look back at our stories we will see our own distinct vocation narratives begin to take shape and the subtle traces of God's presence.

With us from the start

> Before I formed you in the womb, I knew you.
> (Jeremiah 1:5)

A vocation may be entwined with our earliest memories and instincts. I know of priestly colleagues who *always* wanted to follow this path: 'playing at Mass', giving Holy Confectionary to reluctant congregations of friends and family, making vestments out of bed sheets. Oddly enough, I preferred 'playing at schools' and couldn't wait to set tests and homework for my long-suffering pals once we got home from the real thing. Your vocation to teaching may be of this sort. You may be doing the thing you have always wanted to do. Most days will 'feel right' for you because your 'job' has been hardwired into your dreams and plans since those formative years of your childhood. Yours is the kind of vocation described by Jeremiah: God has 'known' this about you since before you came into being and for God 'knowing' is as good as 'being'!

Growing into it

> It was the Lord who carried you, as a man carries
> his child, all along the road you travelled.
> (Deuteronomy 1:31)

Most people find that 'a call to teach' creeps up on them almost unnoticed. There are little fleeting signals that catch the attention but then fade. Maybe a more concrete image is that of the finger of God prodding and poking us in the right direction. We may not always feel the pressure but the cumulative effect of those gentle shoves is to bring us to a sense of being where we are meant to be. If Jeremiah is the model of the 'with us from the start' vocation, then Samuel might serve as an example of this kind of call – or at least of *understanding* the call. Although his mother had dedicated him to the Lord from his birth, God waits until Samuel reaches a certain stage of maturity before calling him directly (1 Samuel 3). It takes a while for Samuel to 'tune in' to the voice of God calling his name in the night. He relies on the more experienced ear of Eli to help him discern the origin and purpose of the call. Perhaps you can identify an Eli in your own story? Maybe the 'guiding hand' took the form of individual teachers whose inspirational presence in your life has led you here – wherever here is. They may even have posed that challenge: have you ever thought about becoming a teacher? The experience of looking back over the years is an occasion of insight but also of reassurance: 'You have called, and here I am.'

Kicking and screaming

> The effort to restrain it wearied me, I could not bear it. (Jeremiah 20:9)

I occasionally meet students and practitioners who tell me of their struggle with their vocation. Rather than something they have been drawn to, the idea of teaching has come unlooked for into their minds and supplanted another dream they had cherished for years. They have usually tried to dismiss the idea but, like Freud's image of the heckler ejected from the public meeting, the 'unwelcome notion' has simply thrown stones at the window from outside. It refuses to go away. Naturally this generates a certain amount of frustration and even anger: 'I was perfectly happy before, thank you. This is not what I need or want right now.' This is very similar to Jeremiah's account of his seduction by God, a dogged assault on his powers of resistance until he can no longer quell 'the fire imprisoned in his bones'. Teachers who have a similar experience of struggle and inner turmoil can often be the very best and most inspirational of teachers. They are not to be confused with those who are unsure if teaching is 'for them' (when it clearly is not) and struggle with this dawning realisation.

'Reluctant prophets' are usually the kind of people who unwittingly attest to God's providential designs. No matter how unlikely a choice they may consider themselves, they are manoeuvred by Christ into realising that no one else can do what they are asked to do. No one else can 'be them' in those circumstances; this is where they are meant to be. The fact that they cannot quite figure 'Why them?' serves to add a rawness and directness to their witness.

What next?

I wonder what became of the woman after Jesus had moved on? It is too easy to speculate but I wonder what changed in her life? The daily trek to the well was almost certainly still a feature of her life but perhaps now, as she lowered her bucket into its depths, she reconnected with that moment when she *truly* saw herself, when the inconsistencies of her life were exposed to the light. We know that she was in a relationship that fell outside the norms of her religion and society. Jesus recognises this inconsistency but does not 'bawl her out' over it. Instead he praises her, encouraging her first steps towards a new life. His attitude is one of understanding; he uses her confession as a way of moving her life on from its current rut. Christ's attitude is an important template for our own attitudes and behaviour. Once they have accepted the truth, people in the woman's situation do not need to be beaten about the head with it.

Implicit in this conversation between Jesus and the woman is the suggestion that she has to be prepared to *do* something about this basic dishonesty in her relationship. Having dredged up some of her deepest longings, Jesus is not prepared to let the woman slip back into her old life and its routines. He senses a thirst for freedom in her but freedom cannot be foisted on anyone. She must take control of her life, no matter how difficult it may be to do so and how much easier the status quo is to maintain. There is a discipline in love (and, obviously, in discipleship). What we see enacted by the well of Sychar is the invitation extended by Saint Benedict in the prologue to his *Rule*:

> L I S T E N carefully, my child,
> to your master's precepts,
> and incline the ear of your heart.
> Receive willingly and carry out effectively
> your loving father's advice,
> that by the labour of obedience
> you may return to Him
> from whom you had departed by the sloth of
> disobedience.

Jesus has listened to her (perhaps in a way she had never been listened to before) and now invites her to 'incline the ear of her heart'. He calls her to shake off the 'sloth of disobedience' and see how she has sleepwalked away from God and her true self. (Sloth is a very apposite way of discussing sin: most of our sins are born of apathy, indifference and laziness. We become mired in stupid, sinful habits because the effort to resist is too much of a tall order. If getting up to look for the remote control handset becomes a daunting and draining prospect, is it likely that I will expend much energy in seeking out my inner path?)

We can only surmise that the woman did indeed embrace the discipline of love and took the necessary steps to change her life. What was true for her is certainly every bit as true for teachers. I am aware that this is an aspect of Catholic teaching which sometimes provokes a little indignation in some quarters.

Why should someone's private life be of any interest to anyone else? Why should the Church be poking her nose into people's affairs? The answer lies in the Gospel: there is no such thing as a completely *private* life. There is no strand of our existence which is hermetically sealed from all the others. No one, no matter what they may tell you, can lead a fully compartmentalised life. The margins of our outer and inner worlds blur all the time: the weariness the woman associated with her public chores was also a symptom of her inner dryness.

Teacher, where do you live?

In order to draw together the threads of these thoughts on vocation and what we are about as teachers, I would like to return to the beginning of John's Gospel. John begins his account of the Good News like a space-opera: you can almost picture the words of his Prologue stretching off into the stars to the accompaniment of an orchestra. This is Big Stuff. No sooner have we heard about the cosmic struggle of light and darkness than the camera zooms dizzyingly onto planet earth for our first glimpse of this Word made flesh...

On the following day as John stood there again with two of his disciples, Jesus passed, and John stared hard at him and said, 'Look, there is the lamb of God'. Hearing this, the two disciples followed Jesus. Jesus turned around, saw them following and said, 'What do you want?' They answered, 'Rabbi,' which means 'teacher', 'Where do you live?' 'Come and see,' he replied; so they went and saw where he lived and stayed with him the rest of that day. It was about the tenth hour. One of these two who became followers of Jesus after hearing what John had said was Andrew, the brother of Simon Peter. Early next morning, Andrew met his brother and said to him, 'We have found the Messiah,' which means the 'Christ', and he took Simon to Jesus. Jesus looked hard at him and said, 'You are Simon son of John; you are to be called Cephas,' meaning 'rock' (John 1:35-42).

In fact this is cheating slightly: our first fleeting glimpse of Jesus is in verse 29 but the effect is the same. The first time we get to see this Word he is walking. This is not, in the way you sometimes see in Gospel films, a procession. He is just walking. John presents this scene in such a literally pedestrian way that it is hard to believe we are reading the same story. We could not be further from the mile-wide lettering of the Prologue; here the story has assumed human proportions. In a sense, it is a pity that we have to wait until the first letter of John for a bridge between these two scenes:

> Something which has existed since the beginning,
> that we have heard,
> and we have seen with our own eyes;
> that we have watched
> and touched with our hands:
> the Word, who is life –
> this is our subject.
> That life was made visible:
> we saw it and we are giving our testimony,
> telling you of the eternal life
> which was with the Father and has been made visible to us. (1 John 1:1-2)

John wants to see that this eternal 'something' has become a 'someone' who can be seen, heard and touched like anyone else. That said, we can never quite get a grip on this figure: although he can be touched, he cannot be held down. The Gospel seems to emphasise this with his first appearances as a dynamic figure on the move. Romano Guardini commented that 'the shape and form of Jesus' being is a passage'.[1]

---

1   *The Inner Life of Jesus*, Sophia Institute Press, 1959.

Although Christ's Gospel début could scarcely be more low-key, something momentous is happening here. John the Baptist singles out this nondescript figure with words pregnant with significance: 'Look, there is the Lamb of God.' We are told earlier in verse 29 that John utters these same words when Jesus enters his field of vision for the first time. We are not even sure to whom he addresses the words. Indeed there is the possibility that, first and foremost, he is talking to *himself*. For some time he has been growing in his understanding of where he fits in this cosmic scheme. He has sensed the rhythms of increase and decrease in his own life and ministry. John understands that his purpose is bound up with this person and that even he, the Lamb, is not exempt from the same pattern of having and letting go. So that 'Look!' is not unlike the woman at the well's exclamation, a cry of discovery and purpose. It is a sense of discovery and purpose he is anxious to share. Here the Baptist reveals himself as more of a John the Teacher. He wants his disciples to see what he sees and so they do. Whether it was the enthusiasm in John's tone or an alignment of all kinds of factors, these disciples look and, strange as it may sound, they fall in love.

Although some might consider this to be stretching things too far, I cannot help reading this passage as a vocational love story. I am convinced that all vocation stories are, on some level, an account of people falling in love with someone or something. This process is all the more emphatic when head and heart 'fire' at the same time. Although Dante's place in literary history is assured by the genius of his *Divine Comedy*, to my mind his single greatest contribution to culture is but a sentence. The poet had loved and admired Beatrice Portinari since he was a child of nine and she a year younger. From the first moment he set eyes on her, Beatrice came to represent a beauty which exceeded the boundaries of this world. It was a kind of sacramental beauty, drawing him into another plane where God's handiwork was clearly visible. A whole ten years passed before he actually got to hear her voice and, when she greeted him one day in passing, a whole new phase of his life opened up. Dante could scarcely describe the wave of love and joy that swept over his life. He managed, however, to distil it into three Latin words: *incipit vita nova* – 'A new life begins'. That, of course, is eloquence in hindsight. Stringing two words together is a feat for any love-struck young man, let alone *three*.

The wonder and the awkwardness of love might lie beneath the curious exchange between Jesus and these disciples of John. Perhaps they too had seen him from a distance, fascinated and excited by the buzz surrounding the new arrival. But now they were following him – *literally* following him – in a way which might have alarmed Jesus if he caught a glimpse of them out the corner of his eye. His question is either profound or the obvious reaction to stalkers: 'What do want?' If that question is meant to provoke an existential response from the disciples it seems to go way over their heads. In what sounds like a mildly panicked, top-of-the-head gambit, they ask 'Rabbi, where do you live?' Jesus' response to their counter-question is gracious and friendly: 'Come and see.'

There is something terribly moving in this scene with its offbeat questions and unexpected invitation. Here we see why Jesus deserves that title of Rabbi. Poorly formulated questions are all part of the learning process. He looks at these two individuals with infinite patience and invites them on a journey. Like all peripatetic Rabbis, if his listeners are struggling to keep up with him, then a request to slow down (in every sense) is expected. But this is not just any Rabbi. John's Gospel is quick to translate the Hebrew word for the benefit of his non-Jewish readership. In choosing the Greek word for teacher ('*didaskalos*'), he is adding a fresh layer of meaning to his portrait of Jesus. The Christ of John's Gospel is clearly a teacher in word and action. His words carry a weight of authority which derives 'from above'. The language and imagery of his teaching is, however, rooted in the lives of ordinary people. It is their experience of life which gives shape to his parables and sermons. There is also a clear teaching content in the 'signs' or 'works' of Jesus. His miraculous interventions in people's lives are meant to speak to them of God's offer of a share in his life. Drawing near to him and drawing life from him are the conditions of realising God's purpose for our lives. Christ's teaching is unambiguously challenging: in order to be transformed we must often come to terms with the 'hard saying' (John 6:60). Yet when we do give ourselves to his words, the effect is amazing. The disciples who accept his invitation come away energised and enthused. They tell Simon, 'We have found the Messiah!' We hear an echo of the Samaritan woman's urgent appeal to 'come and see a man who told me everything I ever did'! In the language of John's Gospel 'going and seeing' are synonymous with coming to faith. Andrew is implicitly inviting his brother to faith in Jesus. The rest, as they say, is history. This time it is Christ who 'looks hard' at Simon and this, in a way, is a statement of 'faith' on his part. Jesus 'believes' in Simon or at least *sees* the person he can become.

What, then, can we as teachers take from this page of the Gospel? Firstly, teachers should be aware of that *affective* dimension to their teaching. At the heart of what we do is our ability to connect with others. In saying 'Yes' to this vocation we are also saying 'Yes' to the countless unforeseen consequences of our agreement. Those disciples had not the faintest idea where that encounter would lead them. In going with Jesus they take the first steps on a journey that will transform their lives. The first and most significant moment is *surrender*. Much is made of the Latin roots of education (*educere* – to draw or lead out). Personally I find the link between education and *seduction* much more interesting:

there is only one letter of a difference between educating and seducing (*seducere*). To seduce someone is to literally lead them with you: persuading them to leave their path and follow yours, or allowing you to lead the way on a path you are walking together. There is no denying, however, that seduction is loaded language. It carries an emotional charge. Those who have been 'seduced' sometimes feel themselves abandoned. Jeremiah gives full vent to his feelings as only he can:

> You have seduced me, O God,
> and I have let myself be seduced.
> You have overpowered me;
> you were the stronger. (Jeremiah 20:7)

Simon, the object of Christ's hard look, will experience something of the same delusion. In Matthew 19:27 he is clearly feeling sorry for himself: 'Look, we have left everything and followed you; what are we to have?' The Gospels give us a healthy insight into the emotional cost of discipleship. It was not always wonderful for Peter. It is not always wonderful for us either. There are moments when we might regret that initial, spontaneous, frankly foolish 'Yes'. Jesus is quick to sense this sadness among his followers and moves to reassure them. No sacrifice is ever in vain. Nothing offered to God with open hands is ever wasted. Or, as my mother has told me on countless occasions, just as she was told by her mother, 'God sees your effort'.

Of course the effort involved in discipleship is not the only source of tension here; Andrew's question points to another. We have noted how Jesus first appears as a blur, as a man on the move. Shortly after this we hear that he does have a home or at least some kind of address where they can spend the rest of the day together. These two ideas rely on a fairly elastic (pun intended) understanding of Jesus. He is radically free, but not a wanderer. He may not be entirely sure 'where next' but he is by no means lost. Although he cuts an energetic figure, setting a mean pace in these first pages of the Gospel, Jesus is far from rootless. He belongs *everywhere* and *somewhere* in particular. This apparent contradiction plays itself out in the lives of teachers: we are called to be forward-thinking and forward-moving, meeting fresh challenges with flexibility and imagination. At the same time, however, we must also be grounded in an identity which gives a sense of consistency and purpose to our responses. No matter how *new* the challenge facing us, our attitude should be shaped by exactly the same kind of apostolic enthusiasm shining through John's account of this first encounter. We too have been called and touched by something which has existed from the beginning: a love which predates the tragedy of sin and selfishness. We have found the Messiah. Or rather he has found us. There might be some who find this contradiction between being simultaneously dynamic while remaining 'tethered' to be too tall an order. And yet this is precisely what Jesus means by 'remaining in his love' (John 15:9-10). This 'remaining' is by no means static or stagnant. There is no sense in which this 'abiding' means the same thing as 'staying put'. Although Jesus commissioned his disciples to go to the ends of the earth, they were to remain in the awareness that he was *with* them and indeed *in* them. The beauty of the final pages of John's Gospel is that his 'Pentecost' is a simple *breathing* on the apostles as they hide out in the upper room. For John, the huddled mass of apostles becomes a Church through the act of inhaling what Christ has exhaled. The Holy Spirit does not merely hover over them but enters into them by breathing the same air as the Risen One. And so John ends the arc of his Gospel narrative with the same love story with which he began: these men who accept his invitation will emerge at the conclusion of this journey as conspirators with

Christ. They become so close to him that they literally *con-spire* – breathe together – as lovers do.

This chapter began with my surmising why the word 'vocation' tended to drop out of educational thinking and writing. If it is indeed true that speaking about teaching in such tender terms sounded out of place in the 1980s, how much more out of place will teaching as seduction and conspiracy sound in today's climate? Yet it is important to insist on the uniquely Christian and Catholic character of such words. Words are important: as John himself suggests, the Word of God ('Love') becomes flesh and our speaking about this word helps reincarnate his love in our times and places. It is a good thing, even if it is also a difficult thing, to speak words such as 'vocation' and 'love' in an educational context with conviction and sincerity. We should not blush in using such terms to describe our purpose in the company of 'princes and governors' or 'education officials and inspectors'.

I think we have to take Andrew's question with us and turn it around on ourselves: '*Teacher, where do I live?*' Is my identity rooted in the apostolic tradition of knowing myself to be chosen and loved by Jesus? Do I 'live' in this awareness and is my response to the daily succession of problems and opportunities moulded by it? One of the biggest challenges for any Christian, let alone any teacher, is the living of a joined-up life. The woman at the well had been living a spectacularly disjointed existence and the tension between the gaps was beginning to tell on her. It is easy to be 'holy' when the going is good. What about when the easy compromises and 'flirtations' of the rest of life come knocking? Do we keep the memory of our calling fresh in our minds or do we allow ourselves to be dazzled by the novelty of other paths and possibilities?

What sets genuine disciples and saints apart from the rest is not that they were miraculously spared the temptation to keep *schtüm* but that they came very close to it and persevered. Although Andrew tends to occupy a much lower billing in all the Gospels (after John's promising start he soon gets eclipsed by his brother), the pious legends surrounding his martyrdom offer us a final little detail which is entirely in keeping with his first appearance. When he is finally brought face-to-face with the instrument of his death, Andrew does not shrink from it but, 'like a lover', clutches the wood of the cross to him. It is like a love letter, long delayed, from Jesus himself. The memory of that first meeting may have flooded back to his mind in those last minutes of his life: 'come and see'. A 'Yes', uttered in youth, had become an 'Amen'. My own prayer (and I make it for everyone holding this book) is that the 'Yes' of our first love for teaching may crystallise in the end into an 'Amen'.

Reflection

Perhaps you could refer to the Spiritual Development Profile *in Part II to help you sketch out your own vocation story as a teacher. Be attentive to the 'significant others' in your story, as well as those experiences – both positive and negative – which have shaped you as a teacher and a person. Foster a vocational outlook on life which looks for God's fingerprints even in the brief, random encounters of everyday life.*

PRAYER
Opening Ourselves to God

Batter my heart, three person'd God; for you as yet but knock, breathe, shine, and seek to mend.
John Donne, Holy Sonnets, xiv

Prayer is a significant feature of classroom life. Children in a Catholic primary school will usually pray at least four times a day. In the secondary school, even though more formal prayers may be restricted to registration, there are several other opportunities to 'touch base' with God. In virtually all these moments of prayer it will be the teacher who takes the lead. It goes without saying that teachers themselves must be people who understand prayer and who live prayer-fully. Of course there is much more to prayer than saying the words printed in a teachers' book or a school diary. In this reflection I would like to share my own thoughts and experiences of prayer, before briefly considering prayer in the classroom.

Prayer: Breath and bread

Prayer is the oxygen of the spiritual life. Without it we become as breathless and pinched as anyone who struggles for air. Given its utter necessity for our lives, it is amazing that prayer can still be regarded as a mystical 'bolt on' in some quarters. I am not a mystic in the common understanding of the word; God does not shower me with manna in the desert of everyday life. If he is trying to pour out a host of graces on me, then I am usually standing in the wrong place at the wrong time. In short, prayer for me is often a matter of foraging for scraps falling from a table of abundance where others are feasting.

Thankfully I am not envious, merely hungry. And perhaps that is the greatest blessing of all since, as some sage pointed out, prayer is also a hunger. It took an awfully long time for this rather basic truth to sink in. I had been carrying around a lot of childish prayer-lore which should have been left behind at the appropriate moment. The call to prayer was associated with a call to a posture. As children, I remember how we would leap to attention at the mention of prayer: hands would be clasped in imitation of little churches and their steeples; eyes clenched shut in a supreme effort at concentration. As a student in seminary, I learned all sorts of new prayer techniques, many of which also involved getting in touch with my body and breathing. Unfortunately, acquiring the 'right' technique came to obscure the whole point of the exercise. I came to despair of nailing the prayer thing until a simple revelation came knocking at the door of my consciousness. I had been barking up the wrong spiritual tree. My ham-fisted attempts at meditation were an exercise in frustration because I realised that I could not sit still. 'Teach us to care and not to care, teach us to sit still', wrote T.S. Eliot. Well, too bad. I just could not sit still – at least not without a sharp blow to the back of the head. Those who counselled me to 'tune in' to the rhythms of my body did not take account of the unpredictable rumblings of my digestive system or the near constant movement of my knees. The root problem was that I could not recollect myself against this soundtrack of pulse and breathing. Only one beat lent itself to my attempts to reflect or pray: the pounding of my feet.

My sense of liberation at this insight was incredible. I no longer felt reined in by one approach to prayer. Now I began to read apparently inconsequential passages of the Gospel in a new 'prayer-light'. Remember John's Gospel, for example, and that first time we get see Jesus. Here he is presented as someone walking: 'Look, there goes the Lamb of God!' exclaims John the Baptist, with all the enthusiasm of a racing commentator who has seen his tip come within sight of the finish. I am also particularly fond of Thomas Merton's choice of scripture for his ordination card, which recalls that 'Enoch walked with God. Then he vanished from sight because God took him' (Genesis 5:24). I find it a comforting thought that God takes those who walk with him, who try to journey through life in his presence.

'Presence' is a key word. According to some, practicing the presence of God is what prayer is all about. No worthwhile conversation can be struck up on one's own. An awareness of God's presence is what rescues our prayer from deteriorating into an empty monologue or the mere recitation of well-rehearsed lines. Sometimes God has to struggle to assert his presence in the lives of 'religious' people (and I mean us). There is a risk that we come to see God as present in our lives because we allow him to be there. We graciously concede God a slot in our day or our week and in doing so we impose limits on God's action in our lives. Every now and again, however, there are moments when God manages to 'batter my heart' and stir me from the sleep of oblivion:

> Then Jacob awoke from his sleep and said, 'Truly, the Lord is in this place *and I never knew it*!' He was afraid and said, 'How awe-inspiring this place is! This is nothing less than a house of God; this is the gate of heaven!' Rising early in the morning, Jacob took the stone he had used for a pillow, and set it up as a monument, pouring oil over the top of it (Genesis 28:16-19).

Jacob was visited by God while all his defences were down. The place where he lay in sleep had become a meeting place with God, an oasis of the divine in the broad terrain of his wanderings. We are uniquely blessed if we can discover such oases in our lives: encounters with God *in* and *through* people and events.

The Catechism of the Catholic Church reminds us that prayer is God's initiative. He tries to draw our gaze to where he may be found, just as he spoke to Moses from the burning bush and made that a patch of holy ground. Beneath the lofty language between them (this is God talking after all!) there is an ease in their conversation: 'the Lord would speak with Moses face to face, as a man speaks to his friend' (Exodus 33:11). But this instance of familiarity does not breed contempt. There are several explosive episodes where the gulf between God and humanity becomes only too obvious. Israel came to read her own history as a catalogue of infidelities and the resultant exile they had to endure was the obvious price. Cliff-hangers such as these made the Chosen People only too aware of their radical dependence on God. As a result they came to regard God in the same way that a spacewalking astronaut looks at the line which tethers him to his ship and gives him air. Even so, there were several points when this life-line seemed about to be cut – but never was. Awareness and acceptance of their need is always a discernible feature of their prayer and indeed *all* prayer.

With empty hands

Even the most lukewarm of believers can be stirred from indifference by an experience of real need. No matter what form it takes – illness, bereavement or plain, simple want – there is nothing quite like a sense of impotence to turn our thoughts towards Omnipotence. I marvel at good people who feel ashamed 'to be bothering God all the time' with their worries. Sometimes we can imagine that God suffers from a peculiarly human defect: the short attention span. Or else, a kind of spiritual prudery has crept in which causes embarrassment at the thought of exposing the nakedness of our need in God's sight. And yet the recognition of *what* we need is absolutely bound up with the recognition of *who* we are. Unless we come before God with nothing in our hands and no contingency plans up our sleeves, we will lose out on that experience of really reaching out to God which runs through the Psalms. Of all the classic definitions of prayer which have been handed down to us, the one which most closely echoes my own experience is the one we find in *The Cloud of Unknowing*. The anonymous author describes prayer as 'a naked intent to penetrate God'. This understanding arises out of a spirituality which saw that only love (not knowledge) could fully get to grips with God. All our desire is refined and focused on God like a carefully aimed dart. Desire – a kind of *eros* – is the driving force; without it we will always fall short of God and our deepest aspirations.

Although he probably would not have recognised it, I feel indebted to F. Scott Fitzgerald for giving me one of the most evocative images of prayer I have ever known. What is more remarkable is that it first caught my attention as a religiously indifferent teenager. Even then, however, it struck a chord that was to resound with more overtly spiritual overtones as the years passed. The scene involves the story's narrator who goes for a starlit stroll and happens upon his mysterious neighbour, Jay Gatsby:

> I didn't call to him, for he gave a sudden intimation that he was content to be alone – he stretched out his arms toward the dark water in a curious way, and, far as I was from him, I could have sworn he was trembling. Involuntarily I

glanced seaward and distinguished nothing
except a single green light, minute and far way,
that might have been the end of a dock. When I
looked once more for Gatsby he had vanished,
and I was alone again in the unquiet darkness.
(*The Great Gatsby*)

Gatsby is a man in love, or at least a man in the grip of
infatuation. That little green light flickering in the darkness
marks the spot where Daisy, the woman of his dreams, lives.
He holds out his hands in a gesture of *longing* and *beckoning*.
All his desire is directed towards her, so much so that the
effort to draw her to him makes him tremble. Ironically, the
first time I read that novel (for an English exam) I was in the
throes of first, mad, hopeless love. The object of my affection
sat a few feet away from me in class. I would cast furtive
glances in her direction during school and spend sleepless
hours thinking about her. One night I found myself standing
at the window, looking through the darkness in the rough
direction of her house. It might have been a trick of the
moonlight, but I could have sworn that a single star hovered,
Bethlehem-like, over my true love's home! For weeks on end
I would lie awake and try to get her to hear my thoughts,
hoping that I too could work my way into *her* dreams. There,
in dreams, I could say all the things I could not find the
courage or the words to say during my waking hours. After
many months I eventually got an invitation to a party in her
house. As it turned out the party came to an abrupt end
when her parents came back unannounced. I took advantage
of my being in her house to give Gatsby's technique one last
try. Leaving my friends to go on ahead, I stood at the bottom
of her garden and reached up to her window (I even
managed the trembling). Sadly Juliet did not come to the
balcony – but her father did appear at the kitchen window
and indicated that I had outstayed my welcome among the

bushes. Although our paths seldom cross, to this day he still gives me funny looks.

Even though this hormonally fuelled telepathy proved ineffective, Gatsby's gesture still touches me. It says something about the nature of desire and how, if focused, it can serve as a spiritual tool. In moments of particular difficulty or dryness, I often find myself adopting Gatsby's outreaching pose – focusing on the light of a sanctuary lamp or candle. When I am alone and know that I will be undisturbed, I find it helps me to reach out with my hands as well as my mind. It is a reminder to me that my hands are empty and I have no one to hold on to except God. In such moments I find it easier to connect with the thoughts and feelings of whoever it was who first cried, 'Do not leave me alone in my distress; come close, there is no one else to help!' (Psalm 21:11). When my burdens weigh down on me, coupled with the worries of my people, I can only gather these needs together and hand them over to God. This is the least articulate prayer I can imagine but it is also the most honest. At times of real need this kind of prayer has taken the place of the vocal prayer I had come to rely on. I had found that words were becoming an end in themselves. I was wasting my time in crafting the best turns-of-phrase, 'tarting up' my prayers. The poverty of all this came home to me when I realised that I was actually becoming distracted by the grammar of what I was saying to God!

Reading back over the past few pages I realise that, in a sense, I have come full circle. My early experiences of prayer (in school at least) were about adopting a prayer posture. As I grew up a little and acquired words, my body got edged out of the equation. Gradually, however, my wordless needful prayer began its rise to prominence in my life. Now I find myself in a happy moment when both words and gestures flow together. Even my public prayer as a priest calls me to stand at the altar and reach out to God with empty

THE LIGHT OF HIS FACE

hands. This gesture also calls to mind Christ's embrace of the cross and his Father's will – all for love. It is his words I speak. My breath becomes his.

Prayer in the classroom (and beyond)

Our children spend so much time in the classroom that it is only natural that prayer should be part of their daily experience. From the earliest stages of school, children are introduced to the habit of talking to God and it is good that they understand God as being eager to hear what they have to say. Sometimes grown-ups can become a little distracted and fractious, making it very tempting to ignore or dismiss the seemingly trivial statements children make. *It must not be this way with God.* Teachers should help children grow in an awareness of God's interest in the small as well as the great events of life (the 'pots and pans' spirituality of Saint Teresa of Avila). Simple, direct language is good enough for God and it is important that children are spared that flowery fixation which bedevilled my own prayer life. The Almighty is not interested in alliteration, no matter how pleased we may feel with ourselves in crafting it.

This 'talking to God' can be done with our inner voice as well as our spoken words. Of course it is important to provide scaffolding for vocal prayer through the hallowed formulas of the Our Father, the Hail Mary and so on. These classic prayers are an essential part of every Catholic's spiritual vocabulary and the earlier children are taught to say and understand them the better. As we will see in the next reflection, such prayers come to our rescue on those difficult occasions when we struggle to find words. There is also a sense in which children (and adults for that matter) can be helped to pray with their feelings. This kind of prayer connects us with that Holy Spirit which 'prays in us with groans beyond the power of speech' (Romans).

Words are not the be all and end all of prayer. Conversing with God is more than simply firing words into the spiritual ether. We believe that God not only hears us but responds as well. A fundamental attitude of prayer is one of attentive listening: the listening heart mentioned earlier in Benedict's Rule expresses that alertness to God's speech in both our thoughts and the events of our lives. This kind of listening is an acquired skill. Becoming comfortable with silence can be an uphill struggle since many people struggle to grow out of the bite-size attention span of childhood. The now-common expectation that everyone will be multi-tasking all the time tends to drown out 'the music of what happens'. In facing the stealthy encroachment on our time, it is all the more crucial to fence off portions of our day when we can turn inwards (and outwards) in prayer. Although I have reservations about using prayer as a classroom management strategy ('this should quieten them down'), there is a sense in which judicious use of a contemplative style of prayer is a way of reclaiming some focus – and not just in an R.E. lesson. What signals do we send about the place of prayer in life if we restrict our experience of it to explicitly 'religious' contexts? Why not pray during a science lesson? Why not thank God for the gift of health and strength before P.E.?

Perhaps the most important lesson we can learn about prayer is that one size does not fit all: some people feel more comfortable with one style of prayer than another. Certain experiences provoke a different kind of response to others. Teachers should be aware of this in their own lives and help children build up a repertoire of approaches to God. Like riding a bike, once learned these habits cannot be unlearned. Once someone learns how to meditate on a scripture passage and *get inside it*, this becomes a transferable skill for the whole of life. Hopefully a person aged eighty will not only recall prayers learned at the age of eight, but will also be able to use the tools acquired in childhood to build upon these

THE LIGHT OF HIS FACE

solid foundations: 'when I was a child I spoke like a child, I thought like a child, I reasoned like a child; when I became a man, I gave up my childish ways' (I Corinthians 13:11). The definition of prayer I learned as a child was the terse statement of the Penny Catechism – 'Prayer is the raising up of the mind and heart to God'. This definition is still echoed in the Catechism of the Catholic Church (and now credited to its originator, Saint John of Damascus) as it begins its exploration of prayer. While it is important to understand the effort which is involved in raising both mind and heart, it is equally necessary for us to see that God is constantly meeting us where we stand. Prayer, then, becomes an opening of the mind of the heart, a clearing of the spiritual approaches. This is a helpful perspective for older students who often find that their preoccupations are seldom focused around explicitly holy stuff. There is, in fact, a 'spirituality of the slammed door': although stressed-out teenagers can try to shut everyone else out, what they are really doing is withdrawing to their private space where God is waiting for them. Waiting to listen as well as speak.

A suggestion ...

In the secondary school, prayer can sometimes get squeezed out by other things. Some teachers, who may be completely unused to the language of prayer, may feel that such things are best left to senior management or the R.E. staff. Although this is understandable, it is a situation best met with resources rather than a blind-eye. A particularly effective practice which operates in some schools is the production of a weekly prayer sheet which can be used by registration teachers. The beauty of this approach is that it draws on the contributions of staff (teaching *and* non-teaching), pupils, parents and associated parishes. The school as a praying community is situated within the context of a wider community of faith. Students get to see how other people –

real people, not just the usual suspects – articulate their relationship with God. There is an example of this among the resources in Part II of this book.

THE ROSARY
When Words Fail Us

There is one song that any mouth can say,
A song that lingers when all singing dies.
Joyce Kilmer, The Rosary

By now I am well prepared for the blank expression on the faces of my students when I begin to talk about the Rosary. For most young(ish) people, if the Rosary had ever been a feature of their prayer repertoire by the time they hit their teens it has undergone something of an eclipse. This happens for a variety of reasons. Many people are (rightly) turned off by the unthinking, unfeeling monotone in which most public recitations of the Rosary are conducted. It is sometimes hard to see how hearts and minds could be raised by a prayer which seldom seems to lift its landing-gear. There is a reason, however, that the Church continues to hold this particular form of prayer in such high esteem. It has taken me a while to appreciate this. If I had to put my finger on the moment when I began to understand the Rosary it would be during the last hours of a saintly little woman in Paisley.

I used to visit this woman each month to bring her Holy Communion and over the years I got to know her quite well. I enjoyed her sprightly banter with the eldest daughter who shared her house and provided constant care for her mother. A fall during the night led to the diagnosis of an untreatable tumour and the mother was moved to the local hospice, where she spent the little time remaining to her. I was aware that she had three other children (I had seen their photographs on the mantle-piece) but I only got to meet them the day before she died. Although she was no longer able to receive the Eucharist, I took the chance to pop in and see her as I was passing. I knew she was very poorly and, as I was going to be away from the parish for a couple of days, I was concerned that I might not get to see her again. As soon as I walked into her room I sensed that all was not well. This was the first time that all four children had been together in the same room for a good number of years and it was a difficult reunion. There appeared to be a division of opinion as to what arrangements were to be made for the inevitable moment of the mother's death. My opening gambit – that their Mum was not dead *yet* and could hear them bickering – at least gave them the opportunity to direct their pent-up feelings at me instead of each other. By now I am used to this kind of reaction: as a freshly ordained priest it was sometimes hard not to take this personally but now I am a little wiser. Thankfully it was their mother who came to my rescue: just as they were about to really turn on me she managed to work her right hand out from underneath the bedcover. Perhaps because it was so unexpected, it was as if this merest of movements had become amplified, as though she were shouting for everyone to be quiet. I noticed that she was holding her Rosary and, albeit almost imperceptibly, she was telling the beads between finger and thumb. What possessed me then I do not know but I suggested that we join with her in saying the Rosary. I experienced a little panic as I realised that I did not have any beads but managed to make a weak little joke about having ten fingers so it would be alright. You could have heard a pin drop (for all the wrong reasons). Still, undeterred, I began the recitation of the glorious mysteries.

To my relief (and I would have to say surprise) one by one the family fell in line. The mother continued to tell her beads, wordlessly but effectively leading us in the rhythms of this prayer. As we reached the end she attempted to bless herself but could no longer raise her hand. I recalled her telling me of the times she would bless them with Holy Water before they headed out the door and suggested that this would be a good time for them to return the favour. All but one of them did (the daughter who lived with her found it too upsetting) and the matriarch settled back into a contented sleep which more or less continued until her death the next day.

I thanked the family for sharing that time with their mother. Somewhat sheepishly, the other three children confessed that the last time they had 'said the Rosary' was at their father's funeral some thirty-five years previously. In that time their relationship with the Church had more or less fallen apart and they had followed paths which led away from the faith of their childhood. 'It just goes to show you,' said her son, 'that it never leaves you. It's in there somewhere.' He was absolutely right and that is, I think, the strength of the Rosary. Some may argue that the constant repetition of the words forms a barrier to truly getting inside the prayer. I would suggest that it is precisely this mantra-like quality which allows people to be carried along by it. The issue for that emotionally exhausted family was that they did not really know how to be together and what to say to each other. In the absence of positive words and feelings, negative sentiments often come more easily to hand. What the Rosary achieved in that fraught moment was little short of miraculous: it took the heat out of that situation and gave them words they could say together. And not just any words. They were able to say words expressive of faith, hope and love. In that moment they were able to reconnect with something that had deeper roots in their memories and lives than the gaps which had opened up between them as a family. It was, in other words, an occasion of grace. More importantly, the moment of grace was prolonged beyond the woman's death and real healing came to that family.

They were happy to talk about what they felt happening to them in that room and they are happy for me to talk about it as well. Their experience perfectly demonstrates the truth in that line of Joyce Kilmer's poem: the Rosary is indeed 'one song that any mouth can say'.

The Rosary is a prayer which can be as sophisticated or as simple as you like. When it is built into a programme of *Lectio Divina*, its identity as a deeply scriptural prayer becomes apparent. Pope John Paul II's addition of five new Mysteries of Light gives the Rosary an even stronger scriptural and theological basis. Even more pertinent to Catholic Teacher Formation, the late Pope was keen to emphasise what the Rosary had to offer children and young people.

To pray the Rosary *for* children, and even more *with* children, training them from their earliest years to experience this daily 'pause for prayer' with the family, is admittedly not the solution to every problem, but it is a spiritual aid which should not be underestimated. It could be objected that the Rosary seems hardly suited to the taste of children and young people of today. However, perhaps the objection is directed to an impoverished method of praying it. Furthermore, without prejudice to the Rosary's basic structure, there is nothing to stop children and young people from praying it – either within the family or in groups – with appropriate symbolic and practical aids to understanding and appreciation. Why not try it? With God's help, a pastoral approach to youth which is positive, impassioned and creative – as shown by the World Youth Days! – is capable of achieving quite remarkable results. If the Rosary is well presented, I am sure that young people will once more surprise adults by the way they make this prayer their own and recite it with the enthusiasm typical of their age group.

The Holy Father encouraged us to be creative in presenting the Rosary to children. This is particularly true in considering the visual aids which children and young people often require to get a hold on the mystery. The *Alive-O* series, which is the agreed Catechetical programme for primary school children in Ireland and Scotland, offers thoughtful suggestions for engaging a class in discovering the Rosary in new ways. A class of younger children might be enthusiastic about making pictures which relate to each of the mysteries, while an older class might benefit from searching for contemporary images which illustrate the events brought to life by the Rosary. Clearly the goal for everyone, however, is that we are able to visualise the mysteries in our own minds. This ancient prayer should fuel the sacred imagination of God's people. In the 'toolkit', which forms the second part of this book, I have had the temerity to offer what I call *The Teacher's Rosary*. Hopefully it will forge a chain of new ideas in your imagination and enable you to find something fresh growing in this neglected garden.

THE SACRAMENTS
Signed, Sealed, Delivered

The General Directory for Catechesis talks of two principal ways of presenting the Church's teaching: the inductive and the deductive. An inductive approach tends to begin with people's lived experience and then works its way up to elaborating the key affirmations of theology and dogma. A deductive approach lays down the theoretical foundations of the Faith and then seeks to illuminate our lives in light of these principles. Although the Directory mentions that the inductive or 'bottom-up' approach most closely resembles the way in which God has revealed the mysteries of the Kingdom to us, it is wrong to think of these methods as being opposed to each other. Both have their place. The best example of this is to be found, I think, in the sacraments.

Whether teachers are involved in sacramental preparation in the primary school or engaged in drawing out the meaning of these signs in the secondary curriculum, there is room for drawing upon both the approaches mentioned above. It must be remembered, however, that teachers themselves should embody these complementary styles. Not only should they be aware of the ways in which God uses the stuff of everyday life to communicate with us, they should also be conversant with the eternal truths which are being communicated. Although every Catholic should be leading a sacramental life, teachers need to be 'up close' to the sacraments as befits people who are leading others on this journey. In this reflection I would invite you to give particular consideration to the meaning of the sacraments in your own life. At various points I will make some suggestions about ways of re-connecting with the sacraments.

One piece of terminology which I have never found particularly attractive is 'administer'. Although it has connotations of 'ministering to' it also brings with it some bureaucratic baggage. The administration of the sacraments conjures up images of managing and applying, things that are done *to* us rather than symbols and actions which awaken and renew something *in* us. My preferred term is 'celebrate', since it bridges the active and passive modes of living and also suggests something joyful. We *celebrate* the steps and transitions of life, sharing the moment with others. In this we follow the example of Jesus who is himself the key sacrament of God: each stage in the unfolding of his life is marked by some event steeped in meaning. He does not emerge unchanged from these experiences but integrates them into his mission and identity. For example, at his baptism in the Jordan Jesus is *signed* by God, marked out as 'the Beloved'. The Spirit comes down upon him like a dove, *sealing* him as the anointed of God. But this anointing is not for his benefit. He sees only too clearly that his purpose is to give his life 'as a ransom for many'. His life is not his own. The basic thrust of the Gospel is the gradual handing over of his life. At his baptism, at the Transfiguration, in the Upper Room, on Golgotha, Christ is *signed, sealed and delivered*. And so are we: we are chosen in him; we are changed with him; we are surrendered to him and delivered by him.

Baptism and confirmation

Baptism is *the* sacrament of new life. Although some families see this event as an opportunity to 'wet the baby's head' in more ways than one, there is still an opening to grace. It is good that families come together to celebrate new life. My own baptism took place in the presence of my two godparents (my sister and my cousin). No one else from my family was there – and this was the norm even in the late 1960s. Perhaps it was the same for you. Given this, I find baptisms an invaluable opportunity to catechise the unusual congregation in front of me. Since most people are absolutely enthralled by this new person who has come into their world, it is easy to turn their attention to what is going on beneath the surface.

Almost everyone struggles to be good and honest. There are times, however, when selfishness asserts itself and occasions of grace go deliberately ignored. These are symptoms of the hangover of original sin. Although the 'stain of Adam's sin' is washed away in the waters of baptism, our nature is left with that woundedness which gives us a 'stitch' in the spiritual race of life. Even though the little people brought forward for baptism are almost uniformly gorgeous and innocent, most families are prepared to acknowledge the flaws in our nature which require life-long healing. It is against this backdrop that the prayer of exorcism loses its potentially menacing overtones and becomes another 'thing' that no parent would knowingly omit from their routine of care – it is right up there with inoculations and baby monitors!

The symbols and gestures of baptism can be made to speak clearly to families. The white robe is not only a symbol of the dignity and innocence of the Christian; it also expresses the love of God which enfolds this new life – and this is something which new mothers and fathers can relate to without difficulty. Anointing their child close to the heart, so that the word of God can seep in and find a home there, strikes a chord in their hearts. Even more so in the anointing with Chrism: to tell them that their child is being signed and sealed with a share in Christ's eternal and undying power excites real pride! There is no title under heaven greater than the one being conferred on their child at that moment – a son or daughter of God. The rite of *Ephphatha*, where the child's mouth and ears are blessed, addresses a concern which every parent knows and gives it a spiritual twist. Echoing Christ's command to 'be open', we are praying not simply that the baby will grow to hear and speak properly but that they will also know what to say, how to say it and stop their ears from hearing lies and gossip.

Before the actual moment of baptism, the parents and godparents are invited to renounce sin and profess faith. Although they are asked to do so explicitly, I usually invite everyone who feels able to do the same. Since there is often at least one video-recorder in the Church, I like to remind the congregation that this is a way of replaying the 'tape' of their own baptism. No longer need this sacrament be seen as something that was done to them but as something which is renewed in them each day. The living water promised to the woman at the well has been poured over us too.

Confirmation is the sacrament most closely linked with baptism. In some areas there has been a concerted effort to underscore this connection by celebrating confirmation *before* a child receives the Eucharist for the first time. This restores the ancient order of the Sacraments of Initiation as observed by the early Church (albeit with adults). A consequence of this change is that confirmation is seen as the sacrament which completes the work of baptism rather than being the sacramental boundary marker of adolescence. One of the drawbacks of this change is that many parents' experience of the sacrament will be significantly different from that of their children. The ideas of spiritual maturity ('growing up into Christ') and self-discipline (the tap on the cheek which was meant to harden the recipient in readiness for the rigours of spiritual combat) are no longer so prominent in the various programmes of Catechetical preparation. Now it is the notion of full membership of the Church which is in the ascendant. Given these shifts of emphasis, class teachers can often feel themselves to be caught in the middle. Their presentation of the sacrament is almost certainly bound up with their own experience of it, and this may lead to some confusion. Given that it is the Sacrament of Holy Communion which actually completes the process of initiation, many teachers are tempted to simply gloss over confirmation and concentrate more on the Eucharist. This is a great pity since what began as the 'Cinderella sacrament' now risks being written out of the show altogether!

Some elements of confirmation remain unchanged and these are worth holding onto as we consider the relevance of this sacrament. No matter what age a person is confirmed, the Holy Spirit is a key player. Even though the Spirit is invoked in every sacrament and saving action of the Church, confirmation gives pride of place to the consoler and advocate. As the bishop (or delegated priest) anoints the candidate on the forehead with chrism, he says, 'Be sealed with the gift of the Holy Spirit'. The Holy Spirit is itself the gift, bringing many other gifts and fruits in train. This simple action is a window of grace allowing the child to experience something of their baptism once again: they will already have re-lit their baptismal candles, professed their faith and been sprinkled with Holy Water. Now they can smell the fragrance of the oil and balsam and feel the touch of the bishop who anoints and the sponsor who supports and sustains: both bishop and sponsor are symbols of the Holy Spirit.

As years pass and the memory of confirmation begins to fade, one thing that almost everyone remembers is their confirmation name. Even spectacularly lapsed Catholics will be able to tell you the name they chose and, with a little cajoling, they may even recall the reason for it. Names are important. In these times (*alas!*) when many children seem to be named after whichever pop or movie star is currently plastered over the front pages of glossy magazines, it can be easy to forget the power of a name. Names were, of course, passed down from one generation to the next. Other names were chosen because of their deeper meaning: many a 'John' has been so-called because the parents have been aware that God in his generosity has made them a gift. In the ancient Hebrew tradition names captured something of a person's essence. Names were not to be treated lightly: especially not the Name of God, which is so holy that it may not be spoken. While God affirms that his name is 'unchanging', he is not averse to changing the names of those who cross his path. The scriptures give us an interesting insight into the connection between someone's name and their true identity. Three particular instances stand out in the *Alive-O* programme (*Alive-O 7*, lesson 10): Abram who becomes Abraham (Genesis 17:5), Jacob who becomes Israel (Genesis 32:27) and Simon, who is nicknamed Cephas or Peter (Matthew 16:18).

The fact that Abram's name gets extended by a syllable is itself significant. He has been told that he will become the father 'of many' and the extension of his line through history is mirrored in the lengthening of his name. Abraham has undergone a radical transformation in his fortune: as a childless man he has been reckoned as good as dead; now he is super-fruitful. His wife Sarai also receives a new name from God – Sarah ('princess'). Her feelings of bitterness and insecurity have been replaced by a sense of wonder at what God has promised her. This change in their identities came about, more or less directly, as a result of their hospitality to three strangers who later turn out to be angels. Although they had no children of their own, they were not closed in upon themselves. The openness they show to others is rewarded by openness to new life.

Jacob's transformation is, if anything, more extreme. He spends a night grappling with a stranger who uses underhand methods to get the better of him. And a man wrestled with him until the breaking of the day. When the man saw that he did not prevail against Jacob, he touched his hip socket, and

Jacob's hip was put out of joint as he wrestled with him. Then he said, 'Let me go, for the day has broken.' But Jacob said, 'I will not let you go unless you bless me.' And he said to him, 'What is your name?' And he said, 'Jacob.' Then he said, 'Your name shall no longer be called Jacob, but Israel, for you have striven with God and with men, and have prevailed.' Then Jacob asked him, 'Please tell me your name.' But he said, 'Why is it that you ask my name?' And there he blessed him (Genesis 32:24-29).

As with the story of Abraham, the stranger is later revealed as a heavenly being and, before releasing him, Jacob asks his blessing. The blessing which follows is actually the bestowal of a new identity: he is no longer 'Jacob' but 'Israel'. His dogged refusal to surrender is recalled in his new name. Every time he was called 'Israel' he would be reminded of that struggle. But Jacob-Israel emerged not only with a new name; he also acquired a limp. He had been physically altered by this encounter with God.

Compared with these 'undercover operations', Simon's renaming seems much more transparent. Jesus asks his disciples, 'Who do people say the Son of Man is?' Simon reports the word on the streets about Jesus: John the Baptist, Elijah or another of the prophets come back to life. It is only when Jesus asks Simon to cut through the hearsay and tell him what *he* thinks, that we hear those ringing words: 'You are the Christ, the Son of the living God' (Matthew 16:16).

Simon is rewarded for nailing his colours (a fairly rare occurrence it must be said) with the nick-name 'Cephas' or 'Rock'. For a brief moment he stepped outside the 'safe' environment of received wisdom and human thinking. God had revealed something of Christ's true identity to Simon (according to Matthew's chronology the Transfiguration is still to come) and, no matter how odd it may have sounded, he came right out with it. It is as though Jesus is showing Simon (or Peter) the strength which comes from boldly accepting God's word and acting upon it. This is made all the more apparent a mere five verses later (Matthew 16:23) when Jesus calls him something altogether less flattering: 'Get behind me, Satan!' Poor Simon. The problem is that he has snapped back into a purely human way of thinking about Christ. At the first mention of rejection and death, Simon reacts with all-too understandable horror: *this must not be allowed to happen to Jesus*. Jesus, however, is far more focused on what he must do and no one must stand in his way. Cephas, the Rock, has become a boulder in his path. Not all name-changes are straightforward.

What these episodes illustrate is that each person who goes into an encounter with God comes out the other side as a different person. In some cases this change of identity is permanent: Abraham is forever the father of a multitude of nations. With Jacob the change was underscored by a physical sign: he would be reminded of God at every step. In Simon's case the change is much more complex. The new identity he has been given must be constantly rediscovered and clung to: it is all too easy for him to slip back into being Simon. It is not really Peter who denies Jesus three times. Rather it is the frightened, inconsistent Simon who caves in under pressure.

Where are we in terms of the identities we assumed at confirmation? Do we continue to value the qualities we aspired to in that choice of name?

The Eucharist

If there is any word which catches the substance of a Catholic teacher's life (or what it should be), then that word is 'Eucharistic'. Not only is the Eucharist 'the source and summit of the Christian life' (*Lumen gentium*, 11), it is the perfect synthesis of the mission and purpose of Catholic Education. Any talk of the sacraments must include a sense of what is happening beneath the surface. This is eminently true of the matter and relationships involved in teaching. Although a curriculum is being delivered and learning is being assessed, there are also implicit messages and unseen interactions taking place. At the heart of the Education, as with the Eucharist, are *communication* and *transformation*.

I regularly invite my students to examine their relationship with the Eucharist as I believe it holds the key to a whole new dimension of their teaching. It is important that they are sacramentally nourished if they are not just to spout chunks of 'Eucharistic facts' at their class. This is not some abstract ritual but a face-to-face encounter with the Risen Christ. If the teacher is passionately 'in love' with the Eucharist, then at least something of this passion should be passed on in the teaching.

Communication is a vital element of the Eucharist as we celebrate it in our community Mass. The first part of the Mass is the Liturgy of the Word, where we listen to God and make some kind of response. But even before the Mass begins we will already have engaged in a series of unspoken gestures: we will have dipped our fingers in Holy Water, genuflected (or bowed) before taking our places and made the sign of the cross. These are the first in a variety of actions which try to express something of our relationship with God and each other. I am quite emphatic about the importance of these gestures: I abhor the 'grudging, hard-man bob' which passes for genuflection in some quarters. The half-hearted 'fly-swat' sign of the cross sets my teeth on edge. We would be quick to pick up on a half-hearted kiss or a less-than-complete embrace: why should God put up with shoddy lip service? Such signs are indicators of just how 'real' our presence at Mass is. Chances are if we are not prepared to pour ourselves into these preliminary rites, then it is very likely that we will be elsewhere for what is to follow. The old adage is still very true: you get back what you put in.

As someone who struggles to find the right balance in preaching, I am only too aware that not every sermon is a riveting exposition of the Word. That said, it is all too easy to criticise someone else. Whenever I hear a student complaining about the quality of the preaching in their parish, I like to issue a challenge: *you do better*. Look at the Gospel and write your own sermon. I think it was Kierkegaard who wrote that the best sermons are overheard. By that I think he meant that sermons are first and foremost a personal response to the challenge of the Gospel. While it is true that good preaching should deliver clear theological nourishment, it also needs a little infusion of personal colour. What we hope to hear is the preacher sharing his own reflections on that challenge offered by the Mystery of Faith; we 'listen in' on what is being said and have the chance to add our own thoughts to the mix. Surely teachers should have no difficulty in setting out their own response to Christ's words and parables? Why not share these thoughts with a class in preparation for the next Sunday?

In the Eucharist we not only *communicate* in the sense of listening and responding, we are also invited to receive the Body and Blood of Christ. This communication is of the most intimate kind imaginable. It suggests the joining of two in one flesh.

The other side of the Eucharistic coin is 'transformation'. What is transformed? The most obvious response to that is the bread and wine which become the Body and Blood of Jesus. Yet there is much more to it than even that miraculous event suggests. When he was Cardinal Ratzinger, the future Pope had a highly developed theology of the Eucharist and it is no surprise that he brought that vision to a million young people during his homily at World Youth Day in Cologne:

> By making the bread into his Body and the wine into his Blood, he anticipates his death, he

accepts it in his heart, and he transforms it into an action of love. What on the outside is simply brutal violence – the Crucifixion – from within becomes an act of total self-giving love. This is the substantial transformation which was accomplished at the Last Supper and was destined to set in motion a series of transformations leading ultimately to the transformation of the world when God will be all in all (cf. I Corinthians 15: 28). In their hearts, people always and everywhere have somehow expected a change, a transformation of the world. Here now is the central act of transformation that alone can truly renew the world: violence is transformed into love, and death into life. Since this act transmutes death into love, death as such is already conquered from within, the Resurrection is already present in it. Death is, so to speak, mortally wounded, so that it can no longer have the last word. To use an image well known to us today, this is like inducing nuclear fission in the very heart of being – the victory of love over hatred, the victory of love over death. Only this intimate explosion of good conquering evil can then trigger off the series of transformations that little by little will change the world.

(*Homily at Marienfeld*, 21 August 2005)

Pope Benedict conjures up the image of a 'chain reaction' of transformation sparked off by Christ's self-sacrificing love. We are, as it were, caught up in the blast. But this transformation is such that it sucks the power from violence and channels it back into love. Love is the key to understanding the change which takes place before us at

Mass. Perhaps it might be helpful to consider love's transforming power in another context: that of two people 'in love'. Falling in love is a thrilling experience – and occasionally a painful one. There can be tremendous uncertainty in wondering if the object of our affection feels the same way. We look for the merest signal, we dissect every word for any hint that something is happening on a deeper level. Then comes the Magic Moment when we either say the words 'I love you' or get to hear them spoken by another. So long as these words are truly meant and gladly received, they bring about a real change in the relationship. Although the change is not visible to the onlooker, something has happened beneath the surface. Two people have taken on a new identity in each other's eyes (if not yet the world's). I hope the parallel with the Eucharist is beginning to emerge.

Through these words, made potent and sacred by the love Christ poured into them, an unseen change takes place in the substance of ordinary things. The most basic ingredients of any meal become the most fundamental requirement for living the Christian life: an encounter with the person of Jesus himself. As Pope Benedict went on to explain in his homily, the closeness of this meeting results in what is basically a kiss. The 'ad-oration' of the Eucharist brings us mouth-to-mouth with God's Son. This is perhaps a far cry from the somewhat dry theology of transubstantiation we have grown accustomed to!

Reconciliation

Most people struggle with the Sacrament of Reconciliation (or Penance, depending on your preference). Even very 'good' Catholics will admit that going to confession can sometimes draw on their reserves of willpower and moral purpose. Part of this is a very human reluctance to face one's own wrongdoing. Occasionally, however, these difficulties can also arise out of our own experience of the sacrament as children. In many ways we were *too* well prepared and the sacramental mindset of an eight-year old can linger into someone's eighties! What emerges in these cases is often a list of faults which smack a little of the playground: 'I was disobedient'. There is a real need for us to 'grow up' in our understanding and celebration of this sacrament. Although there are sinful patterns which keep recurring in our lives, they need to be acknowledged and kept track of as we grow and enter more sophisticated engagements with the world. Dishonesty, for example, can become embedded in our relationships: the sly 'borrowing' of a toy or a biscuit can lead to more subtle lapses in transparency in later life. The way in which we use time and resources (our own and those of others) may need to be opened up to the light of grace.

The 'sense' of sin: 'I am not who I am' (Othello)

If we follow the account of the Fall in Genesis, we see that sin basically enters into human experience through a lethal injection of doubt about who we are in relation to God and each other. All sin, in some shape or other, makes us uncomfortable 'in our own skin'. There is, therefore, an exquisite irony in making the tempter take the form of a serpent which can slough off his skin and grow another and another. In Genesis the serpent asks the woman a trick question, inviting a response which misrepresents God's intentions rather then clarifies them. God wants to keep the woman and the man in ignorance because he is jealous and insecure. He is afraid that, with eyes truly open to reality, they will become God's equal. What is particularly telling is that, in her rush to explain just what God has declared 'off-limits', she actually goes beyond what God really said. At no point did he tell them that they should not *touch* the forbidden fruit. This is all in the woman's head. If she were left to carry on in this line, she would probably end up believing that God said they should not even *look* at it. Although the fruit has not yet been picked, in a sense the Fall is already underway. The woman has fallen for a lie which has de-stabilised her sense of the world and herself. The unthinkable has become reasonable. She has already taken up a position in which her actions are not only justifiable but necessary. Her legitimate development as a person *requires* her to have this knowledge of good and evil. Of course this knowledge is not simply something on the conceptual level. In the Semitic mind, to have knowledge of something is to participate in it. So too to eat something is to take it in to yourself and make it part of you: to eat the fruit of knowing good and evil is to internalise those things so that sinew and soul are permeated by them. Once the fruit is shared two things happen. Firstly, the couple become aware of their nakedness as a sign of separateness rather than oneness. This separateness also affects their connection with God and prompts their rather pathetic attempts to shield themselves from each other's eyes and his. The fracture in their unity is underscored by the way in which the man blames the woman (and therefore God) for this breakdown. An inability to accept responsibility is one of the first side-effects of the original sin. An inability to accept otherness without being threatened by it soon follows (witness the murder of Abel cf Genesis, chapter 4).

The *Alive-O* programme develops this scenario of estrangement in its treatment of sin. Sin is fundamentally a disconnection between the individual and their true self (which is the image and likeness of God). Saint Paul neatly sums up this condition of contrariness:

> I cannot understand my own behaviour. I fail to carry out the things I want to do, and I find myself doing the very things I hate ... Every single time I want to do good it is something evil that comes to hand. In my inmost self I

> dearly love God's Law, but I can see that my
> body follows a different law that battles against
> the law which my reason dictates. (Romans
> 7:15. 21-23)

This disconnectedness also affects our relationships with others introducing jealousy, insecurity and self-interest into our dealings with others. The grace of the sacrament of reconciliation is basically at the service of re-connecting us with God and those around us. But before we can experience healing in our most basic relationships we have to be honest with ourselves. Before we can achieve this re-connection we have to be clear about who we are and what distortions have crept into our lives. This is why the examination of conscience is so central to the meaningful celebration of the sacrament of reconciliation. In a sense it is a matter for regret that the term 'examination' tends to conjure up unpleasant associations. You can fail an examination. Examinations are usually unpleasant experiences, especially when they are a prelude to medical procedures. They are often undignified and occasionally humiliating. Perhaps we need some slightly more liberating terminology which invites us to listen to our inner voice and reclaim our true reflection. No matter what name we find for it, however, we need to take that time to re-clothe ourselves in our 'rightful minds' and put on the attitudes and values which are consistent with who we *really* are. Once we do that, we get a sense of what does and does not fit comfortably in our lives. Inconsistent choices and actions, infidelities great or small, unloving thoughts and words: these are all ways in which we detach ourselves from God's love and 'unplug' ourselves from communion with those around us. It is worthwhile considering the ways in which we help children undertake this reflection on their own lives. The imagery in *Alive-O* is certainly redolent of the Gospel parables of forgiveness and God's active interest in seeking out what is lost. All of us, no matter how old we are, have experiences of getting lost and becoming detached from the flock. As teachers we could do worse than translate the language of the *Alive-O* examen into more adult terms for our own use. In the *Spiritual Development Profile* in the second part of this book, I also suggest the tried-and-tested template of Saint Paul's 'hymn to love' in I Corinthians 13. If sin can be understood as a 'failure to show love' then this well-known passage can be just as challenging as it is comforting.

Marriage and Holy Orders

Although there is no absolute connection between these sacraments, I would like to reflect on the mystery of commitment which lies at the heart of both since they have much to offer our understanding of teaching. Marriage and Holy Orders are *sacraments of calling* and what has been said about the vocational aspect of teaching clearly applies here. We are all on a journey and no matter what 'state of life' we find ourselves in, the Catholic vision is that our journey is one of growing into whatever role God intends us to play. This role is not just for our own flourishing but for the growth and happiness of others. In other words, all sacraments of commitment are about the *transmission of life*. Life can be understood in many ways: in marriage we can understand 'life' both as the beginning of a completely new person as well as the discovery that we are integral to the life of another. Those who have embraced the call to a consecrated ministry also have a vital role to play in communicating grace and a sense of purpose to those entrusted to their care.

Both these sacraments begin with a public celebration which involves the wider community acting as witness to what is offered and received. There is a sense in which marriage and ordination involve a revelation of a new identity, true to the sacrament of Confirmation. Admittedly this revelation can often be of a superficial nature: the way in which a bride, for example, is dressed owes as much to the dictates of fashion as the desire for a new person to be 'unveiled' before God. Even the vesting of a priest can be misread by too great an emphasis on what kind of chasuble he chooses and what this may say about his understanding of his role within the Church. To avoid too shallow a view of these sacraments, perhaps it is safer to focus on what is happening to the *hands* of those involved. Central to the exchange of vows at marriage is the joining of hands, symbolising the joining of two lives 'in one flesh'. This undoing of the Fall is also meant to convey a healing grace to the *touch* which this couple will bestow on each other and, possibly, to future generations. Equally, in the anointing of the priest's hands, there is an evocation of the sacred character of touch. By touching things the priest makes them *alive* and *holy*; in touching sacred things the priest in turn becomes alive with the grace of Christ who makes all things holy.

In the past we have laid great emphasis on blessing the hands of newly qualified teachers: we have asked God to bless them and the work they will do. Over the years the changed climate of education (and society in general) which espouses a 'hands-off' approach to all dealings with children has led many to abandon this practice. This is, I think, a great pity. So much of our lives are lived through our hands and, no matter how circumspect we must be nowadays, so much of a teacher's life is still expressed at this level. A teacher's hands remain a vital channel of communication and instruction and there is no reason why this fact should not be recognised, celebrated and sanctified in some way at the beginning of a life in teaching.

If there is one feature which unites all three vocations (other than service, of course), it is *wisdom*. Wisdom is the key to all love. Wisdom is personified in the Scriptures as the first of God's creations and combines a creative potency with a playful nature. Every truly Christian vocation must keep these aspects in a fruitful tension: being aware of the potency of creativity but doing so with the necessary lightness of touch which shines through every 'grace-ful' person. After I had done her the merest of favours, a parishioner once gave me a little heart-shaped stone as a token of thanks. What struck me was that the word inscribed on the stone was not *love* but *wisdom*. When I discovered that the stone came from a nearby Fair Trade shop, I bought up their supply of these stones and gave them as a gift to each couple I 'married'. I was able to work this stone into my sermon and make the point that the greater part of love was really wisdom and understanding. 'To understand all', as the French proverb goes, 'is to forgive all'. Forgiveness is one of the qualities which every married person, priest and teacher is called to draw upon almost every day – either in their own lives or the lives of others. Another strand of wisdom is the awareness that life holds many suprises in store for us and that the best response to that is not anxiety but trust. To return to the symbolism of the hand, we are invited to 'put our hand into the hand of the man who stands at the gate of the year'. The life of every follower of Christ is lived out under the sign of the cross which is also, for the spiritually alert, the sign of God's providence. Whether we are currently experiencing the 'better or worse' aspects of our commitments, we believe that God is with us through it all.

Reflection

The Sacraments of Commitment involve a public exchange of vows or a making of promises. It is always helpful for married people and priests to revisit these foundational texts of their lives and pray that they will become a source of renewed grace. Other professions, most famously medicine, also require new entrants to swear an Oath and their subsequent conduct is judged against this statement. Although there is no comparable text for teachers, we could perhaps consider the sentiments contained in this prayer we use at Glasgow University:

Lord Jesus, as we leave this place today, teachers starting on their journey, we come to you like the disciples on the Road to Emmaus.

You accompanied them on their journey, you opened their eyes to the truth contained in the Scriptures, you rekindled their hope and you revealed yourself to them in the breaking of the bread.

Like them, we place our trust in you to accompany us as we, fed on your Word and your Body, in our turn, take up the commission to lead your people along the path of discipleship.

Today we renew our trust in you! Open our hearts to your Word.

We ask this in union with the whole Church throughout the world.

We pray that you will find in us souls ready for communion with you, Our Teacher and Provider, and with the young people you have entrusted to our guidance.

You encouraged your disciples by explaining to them the full meaning of the scriptures – that you had to suffer and so enter into your glory. Help us to enkindle the hearts of the young with the wisdom of the Gospel.

You remained with the disciples into the evening upon their request. Teach us to stay close to your children even to the end.

Your disciples recognised you in the breaking of the Bread. Show us how to reveal your saving grace in the kindness of our actions and in the gentle example of faith filled with good deeds.

And may we be authentic teachers of communion so that your little flock may grow in the unity of the one body, and the spaces of your Shepherd's care be extended, so that the whole earth shall flourish in the holy fruit of the Spirit.

We entrust ourselves to your Holy Mother. In the school of Mary, 'woman of the Eucharist, help us to discover anew the 'astonishment' that every encounter with you brings in the Mystery of Your Body and Blood, so that we may be ever fully alive in you.

We ask this in your name.

Amen

Reflection
If you had to compose a set of promises for new teachers, what would you ask of them?

Anointing of the sick

Obviously no discussion of the sacraments, however brief, could omit the sacrament of the anointing of the sick. Although it is probably the least common of the sacraments and certainly the one most removed from classroom experience, it is worth considering the message contained at its heart which is universal. We live in an age which dreads weakness and prefers to draw a veil over suffering. In part this fear arises out of a culture which has an equally morbid fear of *failure* and, in a sense, sickness can be read as a *failure to be healthy*. All of the sacraments tend to adopt a stance which contradicts the prevailing wisdom of the age and this is no exception. The 'sacrament of the sick' consciously acknowledges the fact that people get sick and experience a narrowing of their physical horizons as a result. What is particularly counter-cultural about this sacrament is its refusal to accept the shrinking of the inner horizons of grace and hope. Through it the Church reminds us that *we are allowed to be weak* and that weakness is almost a prerequisite for understanding the Paschal Mystery of Christ's suffering, death and resurrection. Moreover, as Saint Paul told the Church at Corinth:

> To keep me from becoming conceited because of these surpassingly great revelations, there was given me a thorn in my flesh, a messenger of Satan, to torment me. Three times I pleaded with the Lord to take it away from me. But he said to me, 'My grace is sufficient for you, for my power is made perfect in weakness.' Therefore I will boast all the more gladly about my weaknesses, so that Christ's power may rest on me. That is why, for Christ's sake, I delight in weaknesses, in insults, in hardships, in persecutions, in difficulties. For when I am weak, then I am strong. (2 Corinthians 12:7-10)

When we look at the Gospels we see that Jesus is very conscious of the healing dimension of his ministry and, like the sacraments which flow from his actions, he too is unafraid to cross the boundaries of his society's accepted attitudes and practices. Where his contemporaries (and his religion) would have imposed a strictly 'hands-off' approach to the sick and the contaminated, Jesus adopts quite a different manner. Those who have been pushed out to the margins of society through their illnesses and rendered untouchable by the provisions of the Law are openly embraced by him. Leprosy, blood – even death – are not 'off limits' to Christ. The Church takes its cue from Jesus in approaching the hard fact of suffering and illness. Although he had the power to heal at a word, he chose to touch the sick. The sacrament of the sick follows the same template, having the priest lay hands on the sick person. The mere fact of touch, even before it is endowed with spiritual significance, is important for affirming the person who is ill. Touch says, 'You are here and so am I'. Touch is the conductor of presence. The sick person is not pushed out of the picture but becomes the focus of attention and love. What follows is even more emphatic. Not only is the person touched but *anointed* with special oil. This oil is blessed by the bishop and his priests at the Mass of Chrism during Holy Week with these words:

> God of all consolation,
> you chose and sent your Son to heal the world.
> Graciously listen to our prayer of faith:
> send the power of your Holy Spirit, the Consoler,
> into this precious oil, this soothing ointment,
> this rich gift, this fruit of the earth.
>
> Bless this oil and sanctify it for our use.
>
> Make this oil a remedy for all who are anointed with it;
> heal them in body, soul and in spirit,
> and deliver them from every affliction.

As the prayer suggests, oil's healing properties have been celebrated for thousands of years but the Church goes even further in combining it with the most exalted sacramental gesture of anointing the head and the hands. The anointing on the head with the oil of the sick echoes what takes place at baptism, confirmation and the consecration of a bishop; it further recalls the smearing of a newly ordained priest's hands with Chrism in preparation for the offering he is to make at the altar. It is almost as though the Church were reaffirming the dignity of the sick and reminding them that their sickness is a sacred space. Even if they are confined to a bed, their hearts and souls are not. The accoutrements of sickness, whether in the hospital or the home, can become 'holy vessels' at an altar which transforms raw suffering into refined grace. Of course it is easy to be glib about pain while one is shielded from it. In some circumstances it can be very hard to detect the workings of grace as someone we love is literally, sometimes terribly, being taken apart by suffering. And yet, the greater the indignity imposed by sickness, the more urgently we must cling to the gestures which bridge the gap between ugliness and beauty, death and resurrection. Sheila Cassidy, who has experienced her fair share of suffering both as a torture victim and a hospice doctor, emphasises the importance of 'fragrant gestures' in her book *Sharing the Darkness*. In a beautiful chapter entitled 'Precious Spikenard', she reflects on the lovingly extravagant gesture of the woman who anoints Jesus at Bethany. Just as Judas bemoaned the waste of this ointment, there are many who see the care of the frail and the dying as dubious use of resources. Yet whenever we are tempted to write off those who suffer and consign them to out-of-sight margins, the more emphatic should our love be.

Alive-O 6 adopts a similar approach, introducing children to the reality of sickness and the Church's response to it as a healing community. The Church's healing ministry is shown as a direct continuation of Christ's own concern for the sick and his sensitivity to the hidden face of suffering. One of the strengths of the programme is the way in which the class is invited to consider the emotional impact of sickness, acknowledging that sick people and their families often experience fear, loneliness and sadness.

The message for teachers is, I think, one that affirms the legitimate experience of human weakness. Suffering is a fact of life. As *Alive-O* suggests, even fairly young children may have had direct encounters with sickness in their own families. Some children and young people may even have first-hand experience of the sacrament itself (the person I anointed most recently was 14). If handled sensitively, this experience can become a way of deepening a class' understanding of what sickness means for the person who is ill and those who love them. On a more general level, the sacrament makes us aware that God permits us to be weak. We should not be afraid of our failures, so long as we 'nail' those failures to the cross, the symbol of failure transformed into victory. By the same measure, we are invited to get our sin-failures into some sort of perspective. The prayer which accompanies the anointing asks 'may the Lord who frees you from sin, save you and raise you up'. There is a direct connection in sacramental theology between the healing grace of absolution and the saving power of anointing the sick. Both sacraments aim to bring relief to those who are 'heavily burdened' either by guilt or infirmity. Each in its own way seeks to clear a path between the individual and Christ so that, in response to his invitation, they can indeed 'find rest'. This sacramental attitude can – and should – spill over into the way we approach teaching. Mistakes and errors are part of the learning curve: we identify them and move on with that little bit of experiential wisdom to strengthen our understanding and influence how we do things in the future. The same is true of the mistakes we make as teachers (and learners). We should not be ashamed of our fallibility. The real cause for shame is to be so terrified of being found out that we adopt a paranoid mindset around our colleagues and students. In many ways this is also the fruit of original sin 'coming back' on us; the knowledge that we are naked before others leads us to play little games of deception. Worse still, it can provoke a kind of hypocritical and *hypercritical* attention to the weaknesses of others. The Catholic school should rise above this and be, as Jean Vanier says of his l'Arche communities, *places where people can be weak together*.

In this chapter I have tried to share the Church's conviction that the sacraments help us make sense of life. Mundane realities are permeated by grace and become conductors of God's life and love. So too do we when, as teachers and believers, we allow ourselves to become transparent to the light of Christ.

TEACHERS AS LEADERS
Sketching a Spirituality of Catholic Leadership

One of the real growth areas in Educational thinking in recent years has been in the field of leadership. Although few would deny that there are some people who are 'born leaders', there is a general view that most people can learn most (if not all) of the skills required in leadership. In large part these insights have flowed into schools from their original context in the world of commerce and business management. If you look carefully, you can sometimes see where the word 'business' or 'company' has been airbrushed out and 'school' put in its place. In this chapter I would like to sketch out some suggestions for a specifically Catholic understanding of leadership. This is a worthwhile exercise since not only should the leadership of Catholic schools assume a particular quality or flavour, but also *every* Catholic teacher is called to be a leader.

From the outset we should be aware that leadership is not a simple reality: in common with all relationships it is a complex and layered thing. The way in which the Gospel and the great teachers of the Church speak of leadership leave us in no doubt that it is an ambiguous and occasionally troublesome thing. When the mother of James and John came before Jesus to ask for preferential places for her boys, she sparked off a fairly acrimonious tussle among the disciples (c.f. Matthew 20:20-23). Jesus has to wade in to defuse the situation and issues a stern warning that the worldly preoccupation with prestige and position should not be theirs. Even the seemingly more noble aspiration to 'pastoral leadership' brings this stark admonition from Saint Gregory the Great:

No one ventures to teach any art unless he has learned it after deep thought. What rashness is it, then, for the unfit to assume pastoral authority, since the government of souls is the art of arts! They want to be teachers and rulers and they covet superiority to others. Some who are totally unfit have become pastors. (*The Pastoral Rule*, I:1)

That said, *someone* has to lead and, to some extent, we all find ourselves in the position of making choices which affect the lives of others. If we must leave our fingerprints on someone else's life, where are we to look for inspiration so that we might do this both wisely and lovingly? There are literally acres of bookshelves packed with textbooks and motivational guides; for those seeking a faith perspective, however, there are other sources of encouragement and guidance.

Firstly, and this is something we will explore again later, there is scripture. The scriptures are replete with cautionary tales for would-be leaders, as well as shining examples of wisdom in action. Teachers are encouraged to spend time wandering through these sacred pages, entering into the unfolding dramas of Joseph or David. If we truly open ourselves to the word, then we will discover that it has the power to speak to our own unique situations. This is especially true of our conversations with Jesus and those passages in the Gospel where he is seen to act with 'authority'.

Alongside the scriptures, the Church looks to her own teaching office (the 'Magisterium') as a way of interpreting and confronting the vexed questions of twenty-first century life. Although some people tend to see the Magisterium as impersonal and controlling, this is not how the Church sees this crucial aspect of her ministry. Pope John XXIII evoked a more tender understanding when he described the Church as *Mater et Magistra*, 'mother and teacher'. The authority of the Church resides in love. Just as a mother will not leave her child to discover the harmful effects of fire or electrical sockets through casual exploration, so the Church lays down boundaries of love. Instead of being an infringement of our freedom, these limits are meant to ensure we do not become enslaved to the impersonal forces at work in our world. The teaching of the popes, present and past, gives us a good steer on how we as teachers should share this same attitude in our work. If we are looking for a solid and moving reflection on Christian leadership, there is no better place to start than Pope Benedict XVI's homily at the Inaugural Mass of his Pontificate.

Tradition

Those who have been paying attention will have spotted that these sources of inspiration are none other than the classic sources of revelation. If you are expecting me to mention 'Tradition' next, you are not to be disappointed! That said, I would like to approach Tradition from a slightly different angle. Tradition with a capital 'T' usually refers to the collective memory of the Church from its earliest years, when those who had 'hands-on' contact with the apostles were able to fill in the blanks left in scripture about how to *be* the Church. I would like to suggest that tradition for Catholic teachers in the twenty-first century is just as much a matter of 'hands-on' contact, albeit with unlikely apostles. Tradition literally means a 'handing on' of something (in our case 'faith') and this invites us to consider the example of those who have handed the faith on to us. In an earlier chapter I mentioned the genealogy of the Faculty of Education at Glasgow University and in speaking about tradition I have in my mind's eye those grainy photographs of Notre Dame Sisters surrounded by the paraphernalia of science, test-tubes and Petri dishes in some turn-of-the-century laboratory. But these are not the only constituents of tradition. There are also members of my family and that extended network of people who offered me some glimpse into what faith can do: good, loving, sincere people whose faith could 'wipe the floor' with mine. And then there are those truly unlikely individuals who would be amazed to find themselves reckoned among 'my' saints.

Might I be allowed another digression to my High School days? Of the very many outstanding teachers who (literally) graced my formative years, I owe a special debt to my Latin teacher who was called Joe. Joe had something of the *cachet* of a wild child: his *penchant* for jazz trumpet set him apart from his peers. The very fact that I have had recourse to two French words in the space of one descriptive sentence says something of the left-field influence he exerted over his young charges. To this day I can recall with absolute clarity a lesson on Catullus, the occasionally smutty poet of the dying days of Rome's Republic. I was fifteen at the time and, like the rest of the class, was struggling to crack open a notoriously terse couplet:

> *Odi et amo. Quare id faciam, fortasse requiris?*
> *nescio, sed fieri sentio et excrucior.*

As I recall, my translation was workman-like but rather dull: 'I hate and I love: how can this be, perhaps you ask? I do not know but I feel it happening and, eh, it hurts.' I was really struggling with the word '*excrucior*' which is just about untranslatable in modern English. Sensing the struggle, Joe uncharacteristically took up position in front of the class and, with a sweep of his hand indicated the crucifix beside the blackboard. 'To understand "*excrucior*" you have to see what's at the heart of the word. The cross, "*crux*" is at the heart of this guy's pain. He's crucified by his love for this woman.' At that moment lots of little synapses fired in my fifteen-year-old brain and the lesson, and much else besides, was learned. To this day I cannot look at a crucifix without, at some level, the agony of a pre-Christian libertine suggesting itself. I cannot look at the cross without thinking 'love'. That's quite an achievement for a teacher who would consider himself well down the list of theological influences *in hac lacrimarum valle*. I cite this as an example of something else being at work beneath the surface of teaching. This is another example of the sacramentality of teaching (sacramentality with a small 's'). Although I have no doubt it sounds somewhat pretentious, that classroom encounter with Catullus was also a brush with the Word. A spiritual truth was imparted in the guise of grammar: that which had existed from the beginning had entered a classroom in Gourock and left its mark on at least one soul. *That* is what I mean by 'Tradition': the fingerprints of faith left by those who sat in the teacher's chair, even if they would not reckon themselves all that full of it. The faith, that is. What I would like us to reflect upon together is where and how we, as teachers, stand in that chain of Tradition: we have the privileged opportunity to shape lives but, while we may have our eyes focused on the obvious moments of faith formation, it may be the throwaway occasions of grace that stick.

This brings us to one final source of inspiration, namely our own experience of teaching and learning. God is always speaking to us, especially as we pick our way through the choices, encounters and occasional setbacks of everyday life. God speaks to us *about* them and *through* them. Every life is a page of revelation, as it shows us the playing out of God's design for an individual life, in spite of the deviations of sinfulness and the confusion which often besets our changes of direction. In spite of this, perhaps we could ask ourselves *am I keeping track of this journey?* It is no bad idea to keep a log of the highlights – or low points – of the itinerary and what we learn from them.

What does a 'spirituality of leadership' look like?

This area is, as I mentioned, something of a growth area and there are as many outlines as there are individuals: every path in life is unique. There does, however, seem to be a fondness in this particular niche for the number seven. Leaders and effective people seem to have *seven* of everything, just like the sacraments and the deadly sins. Conscious of this, and fairly arbitrarily, I would like to suggest seven components which I think might profitably constitute a spirituality of leadership. If there would be a connecting motif, it would be the example of Saul of Tarsus, or Saint Paul, as he is known to most. Although his significance is sometimes over-stated ('the real founder of Christianity' etc.), no serious consideration of our faith could fail to take account of his influence.

Vision

> Without a vision the people perish. (Proverbs 29:18)

By now this is a fairly well-worn nugget of scriptural wisdom. Without a vision the people will die. *But whose vision?* Of course it is important to have nailed the vision thing, but it goes without saying that not all visions are of equal value. Take Saul, for example. He was someone with a very clear vision of God's plan and his role in its unfolding. It was perfectly obvious to Saul that the Christian sect was a problem to which he was the ideal solution. Perhaps at the back of Saul's mind, itching away like mad, was the thought that everything would be fine if only these deluded followers of the Nazarene could be made to see things aright. This

THE LIGHT OF HIS FACE

conviction probably lent speed and a certain urgency to his feet as he took the highroad to Damascus to sort out the situation. In a sense Saul exemplifies that old wisdom that, if you want to make God laugh, then tell him your plans. Of course what happened went well beyond Saul's script. It was Saul who ended up flat on his back, knocked off his feet by a dazzling encounter with the Light. Persecuting the light is a fairly vain pursuit, like stabbing a torch beam with a stiletto. His ensuing blindness is almost God's way of saying to him, 'Look, Saul, your vision doesn't work any more. You must learn to see in a new way, beginning with the world and your place in it'. In a sense he is made to feel like a child being led by the hand into the city. He himself used the image of a strange re-birth to describe what happened to him: 'it was as though I was born when nobody expected it' (I Corinthians 15:8).

What I think Saint Paul exemplifies is an excessive attachment to *your* vision – a kind of 'visiolatry' in which you idolise your way of seeing things to the exclusion of any other approach. Having only one vision is sometimes just as bad as having no vision at all. Although he was a new man after his conversion (a new leaf underscored by his new, more humble name – *Paulus*, the little guy), Paul continued to struggle with 'visiolatry'. Thankfully he usually surrounded himself with people who knew how to gently challenge him when he was at risk of losing touch with reality. That said, we should not underestimate Paul's spiritual genius and genius is not too strong a word to describe his ability to see connections which others were apt to miss. He was able to encourage younger men like Timothy and Titus to hold fast to their insights and not be discouraged by the dismissive appraisals of their elders and betters. Paul could step 'outside the box' of his culture and invite a slave-owner to interpret his relationship with his runaway property in a new light.

The Catholic teacher in any position of responsibility will know how important vision is but should also be sufficiently humble to know that it might not necessarily be *their* vision which works best in a particular situation. When it comes to the world of education a kind of bi-focal vision is also an invaluable asset: it is good to see what is in front of you but, given that new initiatives come thick and fast, the ability to see the distant horizon is also a tremendous advantage. I often think that policy documents, like supermarket ready meals, should have their sell-by date clearly displayed.

Authority, authenticity and discernment

How can you have a spirituality of authority? Does authority not have more to do with *gravity* than spirituality, with power and pressure than prayer? Of course the answer to this is possibly 'Yes'. Authority understood in narrowly secular terms is often a matter of power, pure and simple. The Gospels offer us a different perspective, especially in their presentation of Christ's authority. There is a radical novelty, or perhaps it is better to say creativity, in the way Jesus exercises authority. His attitude to authority – *exousia* – is marked by the freedom of someone who lives authority from the inside out. He does not need anyone's delegation to act. Everything he does is sanctioned by the fact that *he himself is his message*: he is the author of his own actions and teaching. Saint Paul also came to understand this early on in his career as an apostle. In his days as Saul, he was closely allied with the sources of power and authority. The first time we see him in the Acts of the Apostles he is on the fringes of one of the most powerful and dangerous groups on earth: the righteously indignant mob. From his first steps as cloakroom attendant at an execution, Saul rapidly progresses to a fully qualified inquisitor. Among the prized possessions to hit the dirt on the way to Damascus were his letters of authority to the city's synagogue. Once he had responded to Christ's invitation, one of the first challenges for Paul must have been accepting the loss of status as a respected member of the 'in-group'. In its place, however, he discovered a new sense of authority which flowed from his relationship with Jesus. This marked something of a revolution in Paul's thought: the real stamp of authority arises out of personal relationships.

> Do we need, like some people, letters of recommendation to you or from you? You yourselves are our letter, written on our hearts, known and read by everybody. You show that you are a letter from Christ, the result of our ministry, written not with ink but with the spirit of the living God, not on tablets of stone but on the tablets of human hearts. (2 Corinthians 3:1-3)

What is important to remember is that the 'some people' he refers to in line one includes the artist formerly known as Saul.

Perhaps the two most difficult aspects of exercising any kind of leadership are making decisions for others and making people *want* to do what you are asking of them. Just *how* can I be sure that this is the right path? Discernment is one of the key gifts of the Christian community and Paul identifies the ability to sift the impulses of the heart as one of the charisms of the Holy Spirit (1 Corinthians 12:11). In order to understand the breadth of the challenge of leadership in this regard, I think it is important to go back to the words themselves. The Greek word for discernment, '*diakrisis*', has connotations of discriminating, judging – even doubting. It is significant that judgement should be seen to involve an element of doubt. Surely a healthy measure of self-doubt can only lend wisdom to a decision?

What is perhaps more significant is that the Greek word contains our word 'crisis' at its heart. This suggests that many of our choices have rough edges. It is good to acknowledge that choosing is hard enough for ourselves let alone anyone else. All too often it is easier to drift along without committing to any course of action. But what happens when we *must* make a choice? Here again St Paul has something interesting to say. Earlier in his second letter to the Church at Corinth he writes:

> Do I make my plans in a worldly manner so that in the same breath I say, 'Yes, yes' and 'No, no'? But as surely as God is faithful, our message to you is not 'Yes' and 'No'. For the Son of God, Jesus Christ, who was preached
>
> among you by me and Silas and Timothy, was not 'Yes' and 'No', but in him it has always been 'Yes'. For no matter how many promises God has made, they are 'Yes' in Christ. And so through him the 'Amen' is spoken by us to the glory of God. Now it is God who makes both us and you stand firm in Christ. He anointed us, set his seal of ownership on us, and put his Spirit in our hearts as a deposit, guaranteeing what is to come. (2 Corinthians 1:17-22)

Paul is at pains to point out that he is not making his plans 'in a worldly manner'. Clearly for Paul this 'worldly planning' suggests an inferior kind of discernment, leading to inconsistency and hesitation. He seems to be hinting that a worldly mindset, which loves weighing things up but is at a loss when it comes to spiritual choices. This is where discernment is linked to that quality of spiritual intelligence: the 'spiritually intelligent' person knows that the right option is seldom the safe or prudent one. When it comes to 'pros' and 'cons', the way to flourishing is often the one which has least to commend it. In management terms, there might be an absolute horror of those who lead on a hunch but, viewed from a spiritual perspective, we need to listen to our feelings, or rather what lies *beneath* our feelings. Paul's talk of 'Yes' and 'No' is not just a matter of contradicting ourselves; he puts his finger on the way we often swing between different states of mind and spirit. This is, to use the language of Saint Ignatius' *Spiritual Exercises*, the alternation between consolation and desolation. Whenever we hit upon God's will for us, no matter how difficult it may be for us to live it out, we will experience a sense of peace. This peace flows from an awareness that God's will is the 'true north' of our lives and whenever we align ourselves with it we are filled with a sense of 'rightness'. In contrast, whenever we opt for the 'weather vane' approach to discernment and choose simply according to whichever way the wind is blowing, we will experience an emptiness which leaves us feeling hollow and desolate.

Both St Paul and St Ignatius look to Christ as their pattern of discernment. In that passage from 2 Corinthians, Paul offers us that beautiful reflection on Christ as the 'Amen' or 'Yes' to God. He realises, of course, that although Jesus was always saying 'Yes' to God's will, he did struggle with the implications of that surrender. This is especially true of the defining moment of his life as the Paschal Mystery began to unfold: as Jesus falls on his face before the Father and begs for the cup to be taken away, knowing that it is *his* will that must be done (Mark 14:36). That whole scene demonstrates the *crisis* element of *diakrisis.* Jesus does not want to face 'the hour', at least not yet. His natural dread and sorrow shakes him to the roots of his being and shows itself in this absolute desolation. It is only when he steels himself to embrace what is being asked of him that the storm breaks. Those few words 'it is all over' (Mark 14:41) suggest that the inner turmoil is resolved. What is most affecting about this agony in the garden is that Jesus must say 'Yes' to the Father's 'No'. The cup will not pass. The Son of God must also be the son of Adam in unsaying that other 'No' uttered in the first garden. Yet this is part of faith's symmetry:

> Then He will come, Christ the uncrucified,
> Christ the discrucified, his death undone,
> His agony unmade, his cross dismantled,
> Glad to be so – and the tormented wood
> Will cure its hurt and grow into a tree
> In a green springing corner of young Eden.[1]

This is another example of spiritual leadership being at odds with the secular models in circulation at the moment. The leader is usually seen as a focus of strength and it is seldom that we get to see powerful people suffer (when he had fallen to the knives of his assassins, Julius Caesar covered his face with his toga so that they would be deprived of the sight of his last agony). Yet the Christian leader, modelled on Christ, is expected to suffer. As the letter to the Hebrews makes clear:

> ... it was appropriate that God should make perfect, through suffering, the leader who would take them to their salvation. (Hebrews 2:10)

Hebrews has another insight to offer in opening up Christ's discernment for us:

> Although he was Son, he learnt to *obey* through suffering; but having been made perfect, he

---

1   Edwin Muir, 'The Transfiguration', in *Selected Poems*, Faber and Faber, 2003.

became for all who *obey* him the source of eternal salvation. (Hebrews 5:8-9) [Emphasis added]

Now we would not normally consider Jesus to be the rebellious type, so how are we to understand this learning curve of obedience? The answer lies, I think in the roots of the word itself. Obedience originates in the Latin '*ob-audire*' meaning to *listen well* or *listen deeply*. Once we appreciate this we can more readily understand what the writer of Hebrews is getting at: it is in the deepest pitch of his suffering that Jesus learns to listen and listen *deeply* to his Father. His suffering becomes a kind of prayer in which they communicate through the Holy Spirit. So the heart of obedience is listening. So often when we speak of obedience we get it the other way round: usually it is a matter of telling or being told. The example held out to us in the Gospel is of two 'persons' listening to each other. By the same token, those in positions of leadership should be prepared to listen to their communities (big or small) and ensure that discernment is something they 'do' together. Obedience, like freedom, is a two-way process and it is by respecting the freedom of others that authority, *exousia*, acquires its genuinely Christian character.

Exorcism

I can *hear* your eyebrows arching! *Exorcism*? Surely that sort of thing is the stuff of horror movies or the preserve of highly trained (not to mention holy) priests? Certainly very few teachers would cast themselves in this role, although the challenging behaviour of some children is enough to make them consider the possibility of some diabolic force at work! Still, what really interests me is the relationship between the prayer of exorcism and its most familiar context in the Rite of Baptism. We already looked at it briefly during our discussion of the sacraments. During the first part of the ceremony the celebrant claims the child for the Light and asks God both to drive out the power of evil and heal the wound of original sin. Although the wound is healed, a scar remains; while the toxins are purged, the hangover remains. Our resistance is compromised and this shadow over our nature can impose limits on our being fully alive – and fully ourselves. Baptism (and all the other sacraments for that matter) seeks to reclothe us in the basic integrity of grace. This is an educative process. So what do exorcism and education have in common? Their main point of convergence is a desire to liberate the person within, to lead the person out into real freedom. There is a child of God underneath the distortions of those forces which seek to depersonalise us. The Gospels are replete with accounts of Jesus' struggle with these malignancies which rob their victims of speech and identity. Jesus stands up to these forces wherever and in whatever guise he finds them. There is something clearly diabolic in those forces which exploit our children and young people physically, emotionally and spiritually. More subtly, there are unwholesome forces at work in those trends which manipulate our children into becoming faceless consumers, unable to tell the difference between being and having. And then there are those most dangerous forces which mimic virtue and masquerade as wholesome. This is precisely the scenario we find in John Chapter 8 when Jesus confronts the crowd about their treatment of the woman taken in adultery. They are well and truly high on righteousness and this state of intoxication brings them dangerously close to a fatal accident: fatal for the woman, of course.

Although we rightly revere Jesus as a teacher, he produced no resources – at least not of the written variety. This particular passage is the only evidence we have of Jesus writing anything at all and even here it is as insubstantial as scribbling in the dust. Just what is he writing? It might be nothing more than a doodle to infuriate the crowd baying for blood. '*This* is how seriously I take your posturing and indignation: drawing on the ground is more important to me right now.' Or perhaps he is simply writing her name. The mob refer to her coldly as 'this woman' or as one of a category of sinners, 'women like this'. In their zeal for divine justice they do what God would never do: they take away her identity. She is just a shameful *thing*. Jesus punctuates his challenge to the crowd with more writing on the ground; he is 'upping the ante' but also making them see the murderous hypocrisy of their position. He opens their eyes to this woman as a person. She has sinned, yes, but so have they. Once they have all drifted off, the wind drawn from their moral sails, he turns his attention to her alone. He too calls her 'woman' and this might be an ironic echo of the crowd's contempt or a conscious reference to the 'unfallen world'. Perhaps Jesus is addressing Eve, *the* woman who first fell victim to the seduction of a plausible liar. We should also remember that 'woman' on the lips of Christ is far from impersonal and disrespectful: he uses the same word to address his mother in John 2:4 at the wedding feast in Cana. No matter how we choose to understand this episode, we can agree that Jesus sees the *person* not the label or, worse still, the sin. This is where the teacher can draw particular inspiration from this Gospel. It is all too easy to write off the difficult or challenging child, especially if there is no hint of real contrition. Here we must be on our guard: whenever we see the person before us as a problem, as bad, as beyond help, we are simply taking our place among the crowd. Despite the strain it may place on our reserves of compassion or patience, the teacher must continue to see the child of God under those layers of truculence and defiance. Who knows what 'demons' have taken hold of that young life? Who, but a truly pastoral leader, can come to understand the wounds which have resulted in such scar tissue?

A significant proportion of our young people exhibit the symptoms of our depersonalised age. The unfocused rage they experience often manifests itself in behaviour not unlike that of the Gerasene demoniac in Mark Chapter 5. They howl, shut themselves away, and occasionally gash themselves. A modish fascination with death leads some to 'live among the tombs' in their imagination. Understand that I am not referring to a superficial immersion in the Gothic: this kind of misery has no need for such obvious things as black eyeliner or sepulchral fashion. This kind of alienation and imprisonment afflicts in more subtle ways. The truth, however, is that it does consign people to a kind of death or a half-life. By contrast look at John 11:1-46: although not an exorcism, the raising of Lazarus does serve to illustrate Christ's struggle with *the* impersonal force, death itself. Here too, he calls out the name of his friend, reclaiming him from the tomb. As he stumbles back into the light, Jesus calls for him to be liberated from the trappings of anonymous death: 'Unbind him, let him go free' (John 11:44).

Mary – untier of knots

When it comes to sketching the broad lines of a spirituality of educational leadership, it would be impossible to omit a Marian dimension. No genuine Catholic spirituality can fail to take account of the one who is Mother of the Church and Mother of the Redeemed. Mary represents the ideal parent from a teacher's point of view, advising the servants at Cana to 'do whatever he tells you' (John 2:5). If only we could always rely on that degree of cooperation!

An authentic reverence for Mary is, theologically speaking, the natural response for those who fully appreciate the mystery of human redemption. Of course this redemption is still being worked out in our lives; each of us is called to work with Christ and the Church towards this end. Mary helps us appreciate this renewed humanity and the Church's instinctive appeal to her maternal love is one of the easiest elements of the faith for a child to grasp. The richness of Marian theology and devotion is such that it grows with us. There are always new and sometimes surprising elements to be discovered and celebrated. I am a recent convert to a Marian devotion which flourished in Germany before being transplanted in the rich soil of South America: the devotion to Our Lady, Untier of Knots. On first hearing it might sound a little comical, especially when one finds that the devotion is centred *around* a painting rather than a painting *of* some apparition of the Blessed Virgin. Upon closer inspection, however, one discovers a theologically perceptive devotion which makes the potentially baffling dogma of the Immaculate Conception come alive. It does, in fact, convey a theology of liberation in simple and direct terms.

The iconography of the devotion builds on that of the Immaculate Conception: Mary stands on the serpent and the crescent moon but, instead of the usual posture of hands joined in prayer, her fingers are busy picking at the knots in a long ribbon. The ribbon represents our human nature, wounded and 'knotted' by the kinks of original sin and selfishness. The knots can also, I suppose, be seen as the contortions in our own nature: strangulated love, mangled truth, wisdom bent out of shape. We are all tied up in our own unique ways! As the first of the redeemed, at the pristine end of the ribbon of nature, Mary is engaged in helping us 'go free'. This simple-yet-profound devotion helps us celebrate an optimistic vision of our race and our destiny. The Immaculate Conception is not just a privilege for one soul but the first step in a process of healing and recovery for all of us. As anyone who has ever tried to disentangle Christmas tree lights will know, gentleness and patience are the only guarantee of ultimate success. The same is true of us.

I mention this particular devotion since it strikes me as particularly suited to the teacher at any stage of their career. Aware as we are of our 'knottedness', it does not take long for us to come up against the knots in other people's nature as well. But rather than surrender to cynical resignation, devotions like this remind us that we are links in a chain of grace and resolution.

Virtues: What's in a word?

A final stop on this tour of spiritual leadership must bring us face to face with an old-fashioned word: 'virtues'. As soon as the word appears on the page it seems to drag with it a whole load of baggage from Greek philosophy and Victorian morality. This may account for our reluctance to venture very far in talking about virtues. 'Virtuous' people tend to be caricatures of probity or accidents waiting to happen. The bare mention of virtue seems to imply that you are setting yourself up in some way and, in most people's view, this usually means 'for a fall'. It is no longer safe to talk about virtues and, in their place, we substitute safer words such as 'values'. Our school mission statements are replete with references to Gospel *values*, but how many of them mention education for *virtue*?

Authentic spiritual and pastoral leadership must take the language of virtue seriously. The Christian life is built on virtues: Faith, Hope and Love. There are other virtues which unpack these 'big three' and shape our attitudes to the concrete choices of everyday life. Although the word 'virtue' does sound that anachronistic note of making us 'manly', we should understand that these are the qualities which make us *human*. To be fully alive and thereby glorifying God, as Saint Irenaeus (and *Alive-O*) suggest, we need to be fully human. In an age which tends to regard *making* humanity as something we can do in laboratories according to scientific processes, Christian teachers must insist that humanity is forged by the experience and practice of virtue. It is a measure of how unfashionable this language has become that the last sentence looks as though it had been written by Jane Austen. But surely this is the problem: are we not merely playing with words here? Words come in and out of use all the time, but the substance remains the same, surely? Maybe some new trend will come along and the text generation will be thumbing 'vir2' as frequently as 'l8r'? Somehow I doubt it. Part of being a teacher or a leader of virtue is the awareness that words are important. It is true that in some cases values have fitted fairly neatly into the spaces left by virtues but it is not always the case. Sometimes we have taken ideas or principles and retouched them with gold lettering so that they effectively *become* virtues. The problem is that these principles are sometimes ideologically loaded terms and occasionally at odds with the Gospel. But once they are up there in the gold lettering, it becomes very hard to dissent from them.

One of the principal challenges for the Catholic teacher in the coming generation is the way in which the rules of moral development are being re-written under us. Of course we have been here before. Nearly five hundred years ago Saint Thomas More found himself the victim of an ideological earthquake which sundered English society into barely recognisable chunks. He was left standing on a very slender outcrop. The ground of this change was language: the language of law and government. As an astute lawyer and a master of language, he was amazed at the way in which words were refashioned or given new meanings – all in the interest of giving him less and less ground to make his stand of principled objection. In the end he was brought down by words, false witness admittedly, but enough to topple him. More could, of course, see this coming. In one of his last writings, smuggled out of prison and written in coal, he gives the measure of his opposition to this changed landscape:

Give me the grace good Lord,
to set the world at naught;
to set my mind fast upon Thee
and not to hang upon the blast of men's mouths.

Beneath that picturesque expression 'the blast of men's mouths' lies a rather more prosaic and deadly reality: the rewriting of a language so as to avoid causing offence. It does not matter whether it is More's Sovereign or any contemporary pressure group who are complaining of being offended, wherever we silence our conscience we come very close to flunking one of the key conditions of following Christ:

> If anyone wants to be a follower of mine, let him renounce himself and take up his cross every day and follow me. For anyone who wants to save his life will lose it; but anyone who loses his life for my sake, that man will save it. What gain, then, is it for a man to have won the whole world and to have lost or ruined his very self? For if anyone is ashamed of me and of my words, of him the Son of Man will be ashamed when he comes in his own glory and in the glory of the Father and the holy angels. (Luke 9:23-26)

Words *are* important. Christ's words doubly so. Christian leaders (and therefore Christian teachers) must have a personal relationship with these words to the extent that they become *their* words. It is precisely in this alignment between our words and Christ's that virtue lies. The process of getting there *is* virtue, character-building, soul-making – call it what you will.

Reflection

These leadership characteristics have been selected more or less at random. They are not meant to be prescriptive or exhaustive. In your eyes, what makes a Christian leader?

ALL HUMAN LIFE IS HERE
Relationships in the School

Looking back at my own teacher education, I reckon that the only bits that stuck with me were those which dealt with relationships in the school. This is especially true of relationships with colleagues and parents. Even the apparently facile advice about bringing your own mug to the staffroom has proved to be a lifesaver for many a young teacher and helped avoid no end of fraught confrontation. By and large, one of the uphill struggles for new teachers is realising that schools are microcosms of the world outside the gates and all the pleasures and pressures of life are played out in a concentrated way. Since many of these pressures have to do with 'feelings', this seems an appropriate point to look at these issues and how they influence the kind of relationships we have. I apologise in advance for the fact they these 'feelings' are almost uniformly negative!

Cynicism

> 'Can anything good come out of Nazareth?'
> (John 1:46)

Students and teachers at the start of their career are wisely warned to listen a great deal and say very little. Lurking in some schools are those jaded individuals who take pleasure in bemoaning the deficiencies of the education system, the head teacher or another colleague. More than a few guileless rookies have been drawn into unwise conversations in which such criticisms are aired – and these remarks almost invariably get back to those concerned. The hardened cynic is a curious specimen: in most ways what divides the cynic from the sage is *ecstasy*. Both provide a commentary on the way life appears but the cynic usually fails to realise their own part in the scenario and never quite manages to step beyond it. That is what ecstasy means: the ability to literally step outside of yourself and see things from this changed perspective. Of course the roots of ecstasy are deeply religious. So too, is the antidote to cynicism. On some level the cynic has been wounded. Something in the past has dealt a blow to their idealism, their trust and their capacity to be loved. This third wound is the most painful of all, and often the cause of septic despair. Remember the cynical response of Joseph's brothers: 'Here comes the man of dreams!' (Genesis 37:19) Their inability to accept either Joseph or his dreams has much to do with their father's immoderate doting on one of his sons. Once they have become convinced that they are less loved, anything becomes possible – even murder. The violence which is brewing in them comes to the surface in their words which, as Jesus says, 'flow out of what fills the heart' (Luke 6:45). What we take for a wisecrack can sometimes have a hint of hard steel, a cutting edge. The book of Genesis actually gives us the first cynic in history in the person of Cain, as he fires back the witty response to God's question: 'Am I my brother's keeper?' (Genesis 4:9) It is no coincidence that he is also the first murderer in history. Cain probably felt himself a kind of victim, after being 'passed over' by God in favour of his brother Abel. Once our sense of worth and being loved has been undermined, all sorts of furies can be unleashed.

It might seem a little harsh to lump cynics in the company of the violent and the murderous but what is cynicism if not the killing of dreams and the capacity to share the vision of another? What are those sharp put-downs if not an attempt to wound hope and make someone else feel just as unloved?

What is particularly dangerous about cynicism is that *it affects us all*. Virtually everyone experiences some disappointment, some time when once 'bitten' we have become twice 'shy' of similar enthusiasm. Worse still are those occasions when our own dreams have been put down with such a heavy hand that we react to others with similar vehemence. One of the most tragic aspects of cynicism is the way in which it moulds people in its image. Those who have been handled cynically all too quickly learn to deal with others in a similar way. A kind of institutional cynicism can even be established as 'the way things are' and 'the way things are done'. This is always a lie. No matter how true it may be in reality, such a state of affairs is always radically dishonest. It stops people being themselves in that every person needs to believe in a better future and in their ability to help bring that about.

What does it mean to say that the antidote to cynicism is religious? There is always merit in looking at the Gospels as stories about human relationships healed and restored by grace. In virtually every exchange there is a moment in which someone who has been living a constrained or compromised life is, to use the current vernacular, 'sorted'. This is made possible because one party to the encounter is *perfectly human*. Instead of confronting people, as most of us would, with a list of what is *wrong* with them, Jesus looks with love and puts his finger on what they *lack* (c.f. Mark 10:21). The burden is on him to make them aware of this and, if it is in his gift, to fill this need himself. A beautiful example of this is the way Jesus deals with a cynic in John's Gospel. What is so engaging about this story is the fact that Jesus *wants* this person and this is itself part of the therapy.

We know that John gives a particular flavour to his accounts of the first meeting between Jesus and his followers. Nathaniel is a curious type. Unlike Simon's enthusiastic response to the news that the Messiah had been found, Nathaniel could not be more unfussed if he tried. He's got the Messiah T-shirt, thanks all the same. And just to make sure we know how unimpressed he is, he even throws in the line about Nazareth. (We all know places like Nazareth. Maybe *you* come from 'Nazareth'.) Nathaniel's studied indifference is quite revealing, however: what is he afraid of? Perhaps his reluctance to get worked up lies in a past in which he was the eager cheerleader for a succession of potential Messiahs? Nothing slaps you down quite like disappointment reinforced with ridicule. The reason I think that Nathaniel's cynicism is merely a defence mechanism is the ease with which Jesus penetrates it. Jesus shows he can speak the 'lingo' of cynicism, but not as a native. He can trade wise-cracks with the best of them, sparring with Nathaniel over his transparency ('Here is an Israelite who deserves the name "incapable of deceit"') and managing to land a blow at the same time. The truth is that Nathaniel is *desperate* to be caught. He is like those fugitives from justice who get worn down by life on the run and secretly long to feel that hand on their shoulder, signalling that their time is up. Perhaps the apostle-in-waiting was too proud to give himself up so easily, but was content nevertheless to surrender when he found himself on the 'most wanted' list. Witness the way he goes from surliness to feverish excitement in the space of a few sentences. It did not require any spectacular signs to win Nathaniel over; so much so, in fact, that Jesus feels obliged to promise more substantial offerings to come.

What is most engaging about this particular account is the way in which a bruised soul is healed by attention and affection. Nathaniel is like a flower waiting to open itself to the sun. Life in general, and schools in particular, are full of people who have been bruised but can still blossom.

Sadness

> Those who were sowing in tears will sing when
> they reap. (Psalm 125)

Sadness follows on almost directly from our discussion of
cynicism since, on some level, all cynics are sad. To lose
something – *anything* – is an occasion for regret and the
more we value the lost thing, the greater the sadness. A loss
of idealism, perhaps of hope, is surely one of the most
grievous losses of all?

While sadness can make us look back to what has passed
out of our lives, it also has the power, if unresolved, to cast
a shadow over our future and what we might do with it.
Many of the most inspiring people I have known have also
been through periods of great sadness. What makes them
inspiring is that they have worked through this sadness and
drawn strength from it. By the same measure I *think* I have
met a few people who had all the makings of real greatness
but got so lost in their own grief that their potential died
from lack of light and air. St Paul was certainly attentive to
the effects of sadness in the experience of the young
Churches:

> Now if anybody has made somebody sad, he
> has not done it to me but to you; or to some
> of you at least, since I do not want to be too
> hard on him. It is enough for this person that
> he has been punished in this way by most of
> you. Now, however, you should forgive him
> and encourage him, to keep him from
> becoming so sad as to give up completely. Let
> him know, then, I beg you, that you really do
> love him. (2 Corinthians 2: 5-9)

He very astutely picks up on the link between disappointment and sadness. Disappointment is a kind of sadness which often originates in the self and not, as we often imagine, in the opinions of others. *We* get tired under the weight of our inconsistencies and less-than-spectacular choices. Unless that disappointment is met with a clear response of love and encouragement the temptation is, as Paul suggests, to 'give up'.

A sad fact of life is that so much sadness goes unrecognised and unresolved. And then, from out of nowhere it seems, comes a tidal wave of grief which devastates and disorientates. Although some may dismiss it as an example of typical Catholic morbidity, I believe the Church has her finger on the pulse of something spiritually, theologically and psychologically healthy in celebrating grief in the Liturgical calendar. No sooner are we past the joy of Christmas than we encounter the massacre of innocents: there is also in this feast a recognition of the death of *innocence*. Insecurity, writ large in the mind of Herod, leads to a loss of life – and, in a sense, Herod's own 'life' is lost too. That inability to *accept* and the temptation to *fear* the other results in murder, just as it did in the opening chapters of scripture with its account of lost innocence. Perhaps the high point of the Church's 'grief cycle' is a feast that sometimes gets edged out: Our Lady of Sorrows. The genius of this feast is that it takes seriously the existence of sadness as part of every life, no matter how *blessed* it might be in every other sense. This celebration takes as its cue the words of Simeon to Mary, 'and your own soul a sword shall pierce' (Luke 2:35) and makes us see that the most soul-piercing grief of all is to be helpless in the face of a loved one who is suffering. The impotence of sadness is redeemed by the cross: not just by the one on it but through the experience of those standing around it. We can find the strength to be there because they have been there.

Little communities such as schools often have their disproportionate share of sadness. Perhaps it is precisely because they are smaller and more 'connected' that tragedies are felt more keenly. Teachers must know how to stand close to grief and the grieving, around their own crosses. The loss of a loved one is only the most obvious example of this. Yet there are many more subtle instances of sadness: broken relationships, lost jobs, shattered dreams. Knowing and understanding how these 'deaths' can provoke debilitating (and usually unfocused) sadness in a colleague, child or parent is one of the chief charisms of the ministry of teaching.'

Anger

> He was angry then and refused to go in. (Luke 15:28)

If unresolved grief is one of the great wounds of human life, then misdirected anger must surely be greater still. Anger is, of course, an energy. When channelled appropriately it can effect change, right wrongs and clear the air. Jesus himself is an example of justified and redemptive anger at work. His intolerance of sin (but love of sinners) leads to some splendid outbursts. More often than not, however, anger can seethe and boil away in repressed corners and erupt with unexpected savagery. The great tragedy is that usually the people who are standing nearest 'ground zero' have done little to provoke the resultant firestorm. They just happen to be in the wrong place at the wrong time.

Psychologically speaking, if we may ever speak authoritatively in a psychological sense, grief and anger are twin feelings. Both are the bitter fruit of a kind of powerlessness. We often find that we are not able or allowed to direct our anger at the real cause – dumb luck, The

System, the dead, God – these all appear to be out of range of our deep-seated indignation. (God is actually big enough to absorb the shocks of our frustration and it is better to 'have a go' at God than take it out on some other unfortunate who happens to be around.) The story of the Prodigal Son in Luke 15 is actually full of misdirected anger and resentment. In a way it is the father who is the real target for his sons' anger: in the case of the younger son, it seems that just by *being alive* he is putting limits on his son. His request for an advance on his inheritance is, of course, an anticipation of the old man's death. This is the mute anger of a young man who feels trapped by his boundaries. The elder brother is an even more striking example of repressed rage. He has probably been resenting his own dutiful nature for years, kicking himself for being the 'sap' who always says 'Yes' and can always be relied upon. The fact that his father seems to take him and his work for granted only serves to rub salt in the wound. He really does seem to be angry with everyone but struggles to find a way of expressing it. His angry sulk keeps him outside while the sounds of feasting drift out to him from inside the house. In a few lines Jesus manages to sketch an accurate likeness of every Angry Person in the world: *he will not go in*. A fair sign that someone is being eaten up by anger is their reluctance or inability to fully 'enter into' other people's lives and initiatives. As the movie of old hurts keeps running in their heads, over-rehearsed lines from the past drown out what people are actually saying in the present. A person who is hurt and angry will seldom prove to be a good listener. It is all too easy to dismiss those with 'chips on their shoulders' but in doing that we risk consigning them to the fate of the eternally angry. And Judas is an eloquent example of that. He is the angry disciple: Judas gets so mired in his anger that he misunderstands or wilfully misconstrues almost every word and action of Jesus. Everything feeds into his cycle of disillusionment and betrayal. What heightens the tragedy still further is that, at some point, *Judas loved Christ* as much as (perhaps more than?) the others. What went on in his heart as he edged closer to that empty kiss in Gethsemane? It is especially poignant – and I do not consider it an ironic use of the word – that Jesus still calls him 'friend' (Matthew 26:50).

The parable of the Prodigal Son does not give us a firm conclusion: we have to make up our own minds if the elder son went in or not. We know only too well how the story of Judas ended: 'woe to the man by whom the Son of Man is betrayed! It would have been better for that man if he had never been born' (Matthew 26:24). I have always been troubled by these words and struggled to understand them. Taken at face value, they seem somewhat cruel and one thing that we know about Jesus is that, even in the midst of his own trials, he is still anxious to lessen the suffering of others, not add to it. Perhaps this is an example of Jesus thinking the thoughts of another 'out loud' – in this instance, Judas himself. He does, after all, know what is going on in people's hearts (Luke 25:3) and tends to say as much. Could this explain this curious exchange during the Last Supper? It is, of course, too easy to get lost in games of 'what if' when it comes to the Gospel. No amount of conjecture will help us break through the wall of isolation that poor, sad, angry Judas threw up around himself. What matters, though, is that we should try to confront the anger we meet in others. By 'confront' I am not suggesting that we fight anger with anger: if something needs to be resolved then discuss it calmly and honestly. On those occasions when we suspect that anger from the past is being imported into the present, there too we have to be wise (in knowing when to let it pass) and courageous (in doing whatever needs to be done).

Although in an earlier chapter I wrote of the importance of listening deeply to our feelings, this is not the same as letting our feelings control us. A curious feature of modern life is the speed with which people adopt positions of hurt outrage. We often hear people claim that they are 'too angry to talk about this' or 'too offended to discuss this at the moment'. This anger or offence sometimes masks the fact that people tend to *emote* rather than *reason*, especially when there is some serious soul-searching to be done. Whenever we are reluctant to admit our faults an automatic defence is to hide behind a fog of feelings. I think this temptation is encouraged by the so-called reality shows which afflict day-time viewing schedules. Whenever I see these people screaming at eachother while being restrained by sullen bouncers, I ask myself what kind of *resolution* is being achieved by this spectacle? Is it not simply reinforcing the culture of high-feeling in place of deep-thinking? All this is very far from the perspective offered by the scriptures: 'Come, let us talk this over' (Isaiah 1:18). The Hebrew actually extends the invitation 'let us reason together'. In getting to the roots of conflict, we need to clear a space for facts to make themselves heard over the clamour of feelings.

In the end is hope

These past few pages have been, as promised, a tour of the less picturesque bits of school life. As Ecclesiastes suggests, there is a time for everything in life and there are seasons when we will find ourselves up to our waist (or neck) in sadness, anger or disappointment. It is crucial that we do not allow ourselves to become prisoners of these barren tracts. The Christian response is directed towards the horizon of hope, that forgotten theological virtue. It is easy for us to think in terms of 'faith' or 'love', but 'hope' often seems so insubstantial as to be a mirage. This may be because we associate trust as the partner of *faith* when it is really an aspect of *hope*. As we have looked at these shadow sides of our relationships, there has always been an opening to hope. There is, as Paul reminds us, nothing, *no thing* which can come between us and the love of God made visible and tangible in Jesus:

> Nothing therefore can come between us and the love of Christ, even if we are troubled or worried, or being persecuted, or lacking food or clothes, or being threatened or even attacked. These are the trials through which we triumph, by the power of him who loved us.
>
> For I am certain of this: neither death nor life, no angel, no prince, nothing that exists, nothing still to come, not any power, or height or depth, nor any created thing, can ever come between us and the love of God made visible in Christ Jesus our Lord. (Romans 8:36-38)

Reflection

There are many initiatives to make teachers more aware of the emotional health of students and this is often characterised as well-being. Such steps represent a real advance in creating a more wholesome and nurturing environment in schools. It is equally important that teachers are aware of their own well-being and that this health is understood in spiritual as well as emotional and psychological terms. Just as a physical rash can be symptomatic of emotional stress, whenever our spiritual health is compromised, there can be distinct signs in the other aspects of our personal world. By the same token we have to include prayer among the 'detox' and 'destress' strategies offered to address a lack of well-being.

HEART OF THE WORLD, HEART OF THE SCHOOL

You have put into my heart a marvellous love.
Psalm 15

Children often ask refreshingly direct questions. Although I was the teacher's cherub, I still recall an innocent question of mine causing apoplexy when I pointed to the statue of Jesus in the corner and asked, 'Why is He holding that big strawberry?'

The big strawberry was, of course, the Sacred Heart of Jesus. Back in the mid-1970s most Catholic homes would have had a representation of the Sacred Heart somewhere. My home was no exception. This simply added to my mother's shame when I related that day's adventures to her: 'You said *what?!* What on earth will Miss McEvaddy think?! What kind of pagan house does she think you come from?' It was some time before my rehabilitation was complete. Over the past few years something odd has happened: fewer Catholic homes have a picture of the Sacred Heart on display (I live in a Chapel House and there isn't even one there) and yet, in popular culture at least, this icon has undergone something of a renaissance. The merchandising for Baz Luhrmann's film of *Romeo & Juliet* made generous use of 'sacred heart' iconography and this seems to have sparked interest in a kind of *kitsch-chic*. I was in a slightly bohemian card shop recently which had a whole shelf of Sacred Heart stationery. I experienced a little moment of conflict: would buying them be a Good or Bad Thing – a sign of devotion or complicity with the ironic, post-modern joke?

Although the Sacred Heart may have ended up as something of a joke, this devotion started life as a bold, even risky affirmation of God's love for sinners. Against a backdrop of struggle in seventeenth century France between pessimistic and more hopeful schools of spirituality, Sr Margaret Mary Alacoque received four visions of Christ in which he revealed his ardent love for humanity despite its brokenness. Although she had to endure much hostility (especially within her own community), Margaret persevered in living out the message she had been given. The first image associated with the devotion was a rough sketch of Christ's wounded heart surrounded by flames and surmounted by a crown of thorns. This sketch had been a birthday present for Margaret from the novices of her community in July 1685: our icons and holy pictures have evolved over the centuries from this simple drawing. Just as the image has developed, so too a wide variety of devotional practices and movements have sprung up embracing everything from abstinence from alcohol to 'making the nine Fridays'. While such things may have lodged somewhere in the spiritual consciousness of most Catholics in past generations, they are virtually unknown to most people under the age of thirty. For most people this is 'Granny spirituality'.

And yet, of the very few things of which I am absolutely convinced in life, one dead-cert is the intuitive genius of devotion to the Sacred Heart of Jesus or Divine Love Enfleshed. The more I break out of my own protective shell, the more I come to appreciate the significance of this revelation to saints and sinners alike. Over a period of about five years I was regularly visited ('accosted' would be a more accurate description) by a member of the travelling community who looked to me for an indult to his Lenten pledge of sobriety in order to celebrate St Patrick's Day in proper fashion. In case you thought my earlier reference to 'saints and sinners' implied that this man was in the latter category, let me say that my conversations left me in no doubt that he had a far deeper insight into God's heart than I. Although he had seen the rough edges of life and, in some ways, had helped sharpen them, he described the Sacred Heart in the most beautiful terms imaginable. Looking at this image was, for him, like looking at the 'x-ray' of God's love. Love, for this man, was something that was often hidden in his life and seldom articulated as he would have liked. His own inconsistencies were exposed to the light whenever he looked at the picture of the Sacred Heart stuck, appropriately enough, to the driving mirror of his caravan. He was acutely aware of the journey-aspect of his life and he spoke very movingly of squandering his share of that love by failing to love others. The last time this man sought me out this particular analogy had taken on a particular resonance as he had just been recalled to investigate a shadow on an x-ray of his own. I do not know if his non-appearance the next year was due to the fact I had successfully talked him out of the indult or if there was a more sinister reason. No matter what became of this fellow traveller, I find the x-ray metaphor both helpful and fruitful. We have grown up in an age which is rightly suspicious of those (especially public figures) who wear their hearts on their sleeves. How much more should we be wary of a God who wears his heart on his tunic?

Like water I am poured out. (Psalm 22:14)

The truth is that this devotion, properly understood, is about as far from saccharine as it is possible to get. Devotion to the Sacred Heart is rooted in singularly dramatic – indeed traumatic – circumstances: the Passion of Christ itself. Throughout the Gospels Jesus makes repeated reference to the heart. He expresses that distinctly Jewish understanding of humanity which sees the heart as the seat of judgement as well as the emotions. What or who a person *is* depends on the condition of their heart: 'a man's words flow out of what fills his heart' (Matthew 12:34). The heart is the battleground between good and evil, especially that subtle evil which likes to masquerade as virtue. It is this hypocritical tendency which draws the most persistent fire from Jesus, particularly towards the otherwise commendable Pharisees. He, on the other hand, is keen to emphasise that his example can be trusted because he is 'meek and humble of heart' (Matthew 11:29). His radical humility will be shown in his readiness to accept death, 'even death on a cross' (Philippians 2:8) – the most accursed and humiliating of ends. The piercing of his heart by the centurion's lance is to take on both Messianic and sacramental significance as the early Church re-read his suffering and death in the light of Easter. They would indeed 'look on him whom they had pierced' (Zechariah 12:9) and see signs of baptism and the Eucharist flowing from his side. Perhaps just as significantly, though more often overlooked, is the heart of Jesus as the place in which the law of self-emptying is inscribed.

> Have this mind among yourselves, which is
> yours in Christ Jesus,
> who, though he was in the form of God,
> did not count equality with God a thing to be
> grasped, but emptied himself, taking the form
> of a servant,
> being born in the likeness of men.
> And being found in human form he humbled
> himself and became obedient unto death,
> even death on a cross. (Philippians 2:5-9)

St Paul presents this emptying of self (*kenosis*) as the key to entering into the mystery of Christ. The whole story, from beginning to end, is one of a God who is constantly stripping himself of power and glory. And it is this same mind (or heart) that should be among Christ's followers. The only thing Jesus really insists upon is that his disciples should embrace the cross with a loving and hopeful heart. The cross is, in geometry, a pattern by which things can be divided and separated. But it is also a sign of *addition*: if we follow the law of self-emptying, what we might lose is far outweighed by what we gain.

If you look directly at the image or icon of the Sacred Heart, you are indirectly looking at the crucifix. A closer examination of the heart of Jesus in the picture reveals a little cross wreathed in flame. But that is only the most obvious presence of the cross itself. Jesus himself is an icon of the cross, shown as he is with the marks of his Passion clearly visible. He stands before us in much the same way as he stood before the disciples on that first Easter day. This is the Risen Christ, 'who was dead but is to live forever' (Revelation 1:18). Why he should choose to retain his wounds is a mystery for us to ponder. We know that elsewhere in the post-Easter accounts Jesus appears as a new man whose identity only becomes apparent after he says or does something that simply yells 'Jesus!' at his disciples. He seems anxious to show the Eleven, especially Thomas, that it really *is* him; he has gone through the doors of death and kicked them down from the other side. He is not some bloodless apparition sent to haunt them but their teacher come back with the greatest lesson of all – that there is a kind of believing which goes beyond seeing. Although they have been privileged to hear, see and touch the flesh of the Word, there is an even greater happiness in store for those who will bear witness to what they have not seen. And like any scar, they are a reminder of the consequences of an action. Jesus may have been *transfigured* by the Resurrection, but he is able to show how he was *disfigured* by hatred and rejection.

There is a further sense in which the wounds of Christ have an important message to convey to us. These marks are the signature of the Covenant which Jesus seals with his own body. The suffering and death of Jesus underwrite the Promise God is making to his people: if they follow Christ's example they will share his life, his victory, forever. One of the significant strands of devotion to the Sacred Heart is this idea of Covenant and Promise. The first revelation to Saint Margaret Mary in 1673 placed considerable emphasis on Christ pledging himself to us as the faithful one. What we promise or offer in return is of much less importance. In fact, one of the drawbacks of Sacred Heart devotion is the ease with which it can be reduced to a mechanical, 'autoteller' spirituality. Many people are rightly put off by the *quid pro quo* overtones: Jesus doesn't need his back scratched, even if we do. What the pledge aspect of this devotion is really getting at is that the path to wholeness requires some effort, some renouncing of self, a readiness to unplug oneself from the toxic drip of modern life. As such, this devotion is eminently New Testament in its inspiration. If the Word becomes flesh (and God's pre-eminent word is 'love'), then all genuine spirituality should have an incarnational aspect. We should show our love in practice, we should put substance into warm words. That is what devotion means, after all: far from being simply a thing we 'do' in our Churches, devotion is an expression of love in response to the God of the Covenant. It is always to our advantage to be *devout* (again, a much misunderstood and maligned word) but the fruit of devotion must be seen in the lives of others. Covenants and promises are about enrichment. Whenever we talk of love we must, as Pope Benedict reminded us in his first encyclical, remember that charity is the way Christians translate the word into action. As schools engage with the ideals of global citizenship and our children continue to respond with amazing generosity to the needs of the developing world, it is important that there is an underpinning spirituality to all of this. We do not have to reinvent the wheel; the icon of the Sacred Heart is an image of blessing for such emerging 'devotions' to the poor and suffering.

Educating in the desert

Although I love the human intrigue of Genesis and the brutal honesty of Job, there is something deeply appealing about the prophecies of Hosea. His reading of his own life, especially his broken-heartedness at being abandoned by his wife, is prophecy in the truest sense. He is 'telling forth' what has happened to him and showing something of God's self-revelation in the process. The desert looms large in the biblical imagination, sometimes as a place of fear and disorientation, at other times as a place of encounter. It is this sense in which Hosea portrays the wilderness. Using seductive language not at all dissimilar from Jeremiah, he speaks of God 'luring' his people into the wilderness:

> I am going to lure her
> and lead her out into the wilderness
> and speak to her heart ...
> There she will respond to me as she did when
> she was young. (Hosea 2:14-15)

This 'leading out' has as much to do with education as seduction – a play on words I mentioned at the beginning of these reflections. God himself is the teacher who wants to speak to the heart and mind of his people. He means to filter out the background crackle of distractions and competing sounds so that the only voice to be heard is his. He wants to remind his people, his 'beloved', of what they already know but act as though they had forgotten: his love is undying. And yet, hard as it may be for us to get a handle on this, God is *wounded* by our failure to respond to his overtures of love. The broken-hearted prophet speaks for a wounded God.

In this sense the icon of the Sacred Heart could have been painted by Hosea himself. The heart on fire encircled by thorns is the expression of God's passion. Christ's heart is the heart of God which finds it easier to stop beating, to stop *living*, than to stop loving. This heart is also a kind of desert, a meeting place between God and humanity. The burning heart recalls the burning bush in the wilderness which drew Moses to meet the God of his fathers. Just as the bush was not consumed, so the heart of God, revealed by Christ, is an inexhaustible source of love. In the same way that Moses was told to take off his shoes in recognition of that holy ground, so the heart of Jesus – and by extension every heart – is a sacred space. Every heart should be handled with reverence and care. Unfortunately, it is not always so.

Although a venerable iconographic tradition depicting Christ as teacher already exists, I would suggest that the Sacred Heart is of even greater relevance to teachers of the twenty-first century. While Christ the Teacher holds a book (and books are important), the Divine Love Enfleshed points to his heart. *That* is where we find the answer to our questions. The teacher's business is to love. 'Without affection there is no education', wrote St John Bosco, and one of the main obstacles to education – from primary right through to university – is the awful feeling of not being loved. As Hosea puts it with one finger, as always, on the spiritual pulse of his people, God promises to love the 'Unloved' (Hosea 2:23). Who are the 'Unloved'? They are, in fact, the Chosen People – the most loved on earth. But estrangement, whatever brings it about, does funny things to people, resulting in that crippling sense of being unwanted, unregarded, worthless. The prophet is addressing words of challenge and comfort to a people who feel as though they have been adrift from God and the former security of their relationship. More specifically, the Unloved are those people who fall between the cracks of life. God declares a special love for all those who get walked past in the street or stared at for being unlike the rest. The poor, the marginalised, the sick in mind, soul or body are *Loved*. While St Augustine divided the world into two 'camps' or cities, the City of God and the worldly city, increasingly the constituencies of modern life are the Loved and the Unloved. The consequences of feeling unloved are impossible to measure but they have a real impact on even very young lives. Although the *Alive-O* programme seeks to build upon children's experience of being loved by parents and others, as a way of opening the child to an awareness of being loved by God, this 'first love' can no longer be taken for granted. A growing number of children and young people no longer have an experience of being loved unconditionally and this *must* have implications for their spiritual development. Nor is this deprivation to be associated with material poverty: at times in my ministry I have found myself an 'apostle to the genteel' and here too there have been instances of real emotional poverty. All sorts of material love substitutes are offered: money, clothes and all manner of 'gear' in place of attention and affection. There might be mono-block in the driveway, foreign holidays and promising careers in the offing, but these cannot compensate for an absence at the heart of family life. By the time some families have woken up to the emotional sacrifices they are making in the interests of worldly success, it is already too late. Their children are disconnected and, albeit with polite accents, their words and actions are often expressive of deep resentment and anger.

Teachers at every stage of their career have a part to play in addressing these challenges. Younger teachers may have to ask themselves whether they truly *feel* and *know* themselves to be among the Loved. More senior teachers, especially those who are parents themselves, might wish to reflect on their relationships with their own families. Is there a real presence at the heart of their homes? A good, if cosmetic, starting place would be a rediscovery of the Sacred Heart in our classrooms and homes. The plaster strawberry-hearts of yesteryear should perhaps be allowed to remain there. I mentioned at the beginning of this chapter that there is no icon or image of the Sacred Heart 'enthroned' in our Chapel House – although I did come across one in a cupboard downstairs. Of course we have an abundance of other holy pictures but something niggles about the absence of this particular image. There are, of course, less sentimental yet wholly faithful ways of representing the Sacred Heart. Perhaps these or indeed any icon of Jesus could find its way into our life and work spaces. As I have tried to point out throughout this book, there is sacramentality in looking: *we* are looked at and scrutinised, not just the art. In the act of looking we are opened to that 'x-ray' of grace. If we managed to overcome the interior design challenge and actually got around to restoring this key image to a place of prominence in our homes, every glance would be a potential encounter. Every time our eye connected with those fingers pointing to a fiery heart, we would be reminded of our vocation 'to love Unloved'. The Unloved in our midst are those children and young people who have not yet been 'looked into shape' as St Bernadette was by the 'merciful eyes' of Mary at Massabielle. It is not just Bernadette who experienced the transforming power of a look. Although I instinctively recoil from the 'cheesy' side of religion, I must confess that I frequently lapse into a kind of 'cheese-lite' when it comes to making eye-contact with Christ. Given the unusual circumstances of the Incarnation and the way our conventional 'who does this baby look like?' goes out the window, I like the idea that Jesus has his mother's eyes. The 'eyes of mercy' are inherited by Jesus and it does not matter what colour they are. They were turned towards Margaret

Mary, the visionary of the Sacred Heart. She was looked into just as much as Jesus allowed himself to be penetrated by her gaze. For me one of the most remarkable aspects of the whole revelation of this Sacred Heart comes at the very end. A tiny footnote that frequently gets overlooked is that, at the end of her life and the end of her exposure to this vision, it was remarked that 'she had become quite beautiful'. This is not the grudging *'quite* beautiful' but the expression of wonder at a transformation from the inside out. This observation made by one of Margaret's sisters in religion throws open a window to the whole mystery of love: love makes us lovely; beauty makes us beautiful. It is almost as if Margaret Mary, like someone seeking an extra dose of sunlight, had been sitting in front of one of those lamps which stave off the effects of winter sadness. Touched by the rays of a contagious beauty, she had been not only warmed but transformed by Christ who saw *her*.

Every teacher is a saviour

The Sacred Heart is the portrait of a Big Brother. Not the all-seeing, intrusive BB of George Orwell but the first-born son of the Covenant whose duty encompasses the ransom of younger siblings fallen into the hands of enemies and bandits. Our understanding of being 'saved', 'redeemed' or literally 'bought back' lie in the family circle of the Old Testament. It is this same role which Jesus takes on for the whole of humanity, as 'the first of many brothers'. Jesus calls every teacher to step into this role. Just as we are in the business of *love*, so we are in the business of *freedom*.

Jesus is freedom. His teaching has that authority of freedom behind it, the freedom to do whatever you choose. But this freedom is always coupled with the truth – it is truth which sets us free (John 8:32). We cannot be in denial of the truth and be free at the same time. That is why many of the most striking passages of the Gospel turn on the choice Jesus offers those who come looking for freedom or a fresh start. He gets them to confront the truth about themselves and nudges them to take the first, decisive and often terrifying step towards freedom. I often think of Christ as the 'midwife of freedom'. To my mind this graphic but effective image conveys something of the pushing and sweating involved in breaking out of an old skin into a new way of living. But by far the most exciting aspect of this project is that it is not just a matter of being set free *from* any number of fears, lies and constraints, but the proposal of being free *for* Jesus and the life he breathes into us. Of course this all sounds very hopeful. The reality, however, is that many of our young people are so beset by fears and insecurities that they cannot yet begin to make that journey into freedom. Worse still, it is not as though *we* are immune from the same pressures. Before we can live out the vocation of liberator we must have faced our fears and we must continue to assert our freedom in the face of those temptations to backslide into unfreedom. A condition of the quality of our pastoral care ('pastoral love' is a better, more Gospel-centred way of putting it) is the extent to which we feel loved by Christ. Knowing this most basic 'truth' is the key to this radical freedom. I think that St Teresa of Avila hit upon the best formulation of this experience when she quoted the Latin translation of Psalm 118: *'dilatasti cor meum'*. Literally, this means 'you made my heart bigger'. A more poetic rendition is given in the Liturgy of the Hours, where it becomes 'you give freedom to my heart'. Both the literal and the liberal translations have something useful to say. The encounter with Christ goes to the very heart of our identity as disciples. He does indeed enlarge our hearts, increasing their capacity for love and it is in this act of 'dilating' our hearts that we become truly free. We are free to love in a new way – with hearts which have room for one more, and another, and yet another after that. Divine Love points once again to the centrality of his heart

THE LIGHT OF HIS FACE

and ours, as though saying 'Freedom, wisdom, truth: they all begin *here*.'

Reflection

The Sacred Heart is an eloquent icon of Divine Love but there are many other images which speak to us of the inexhaustible mystery of Christ. The images we have stored in our hearts and minds have an important role to play in determining the kind of relationship we have with God and Jesus in prayer. When you speak or hear the name 'Jesus', is there a particular face which answers the summons? The Good Shepherd or the Suffering Servant? The youthful Jesus or the risen Christ? What do these faces say about your faith? Indeed what do they say about you?

PART II

A SUGGESTED PROGRAMME AND RESOURCES

CATHOLIC TEACHER FORMATION

A vision of Catholic education

'Catholic schools are at the heart of the Church's mission in the service of society. The promotion of the human person is the goal of the Catholic School.' *(The Catholic School on the Threshold of the Third Millennium)*

'Catholic schools work to foster the Christian understanding of the human person as made in the image and likeness of God. We nurture the human wholeness of each pupil to play a full role in society fully human and fully alive for self and others, providing a community in which faith, culture and life are brought into harmony.' *(Religious Dimensions of Education in a Catholic School)*

Catholic Education is a spiritual process which is life-affirming and values based.

I have come that you might have life, and have it to the full. (John 10:10)

The calling of the teacher
Teaching is both vocation and profession.

> 'Teaching has an extraordinary moral depth and is one of humanity's excellent and creative activities, for the teacher does not write on inanimate material, but on the very spirits of human beings.'
> (*The Catholic School on the Threshold of the Third Millennium*)

Teachers are: Agents of transformation; inspirers of wonder; encouragers of potential; messengers of meaning; nurturers of witnesses; healers of fear; prophets to the nation; co-creators with God.

I am the Way, the Truth and the Life. (John 14:6)

How to use this profile
This profile is intended to help you arrive at a deeper understanding of your development as a person and as a Catholic teacher. It is meant to be used in conjunction with the *Catholic Teacher Formation Forward Planner,* which should be your companion on the journey through this year. You might like to keep a spiritual journal which you fill in from time to time; perhaps you might wish to share your thoughts with another person – the choice is yours. It is not meant to be a 'one-off' document but a tool for growth. Remember that people tend to develop their spiritual lives by way of 'spiral depth', coming back to some areas over and over again rather than simply growing 'onwards and upwards'.

Your identity

> Who do people say I am? Who do you say I am?
> (c.f. Matthew 16:13)

Before we can answer questions about *what* we do, we have to know w*ho* we are. Our identities are made up of the relationships, commitments and duties we have in our lives. Are you clear about who you are? Pray about this.

Your *vocation* as a teacher

The reflections on the above describe teachers as 'agents of transformation, inspirers of wonder' etc. Do you strongly identify with any of these ideas? How would you try to live out these values in a practical setting? Teaching is both vocation and profession. God calls us in different ways: sometimes he uses the inspiring example of teachers we have known; a vocation can also 'grow on us' as, bit by bit, we become aware that this is where we should be going in life. That way, we can often look back at our lives and see God's fingerprints at various points in our own stories. How did your vocation to teaching come about?

Your role and *witness* as a Catholic teacher

The Charter for Catholic Schools in Scotland sets out the key characteristics of our schools. It also suggests the kind of commitment expected of those who teach in Catholic schools. Are there areas where you need to strengthen your commitment? What *concrete steps* are you going to take? Are there questions or concerns you have about your identity as a Catholic teacher? From whom are you are going to seek advice and help? Remember that Jesus sent the first teachers (the disciples) out *in pairs*: no one is expected to make the journey alone. We all need the help of caring and wise advisers.

Examine your conscience

Read these famous words of St Paul. From verse 4 onwards, where it says 'love', put your own name and see how true the statement reads.

> If I could speak in any language in heaven or on earth but didn't love others, I would only be making meaningless noise like a loud gong or a clanging cymbal.[2] If I had the gift of prophecy, and if I knew all the mysteries of the future and knew everything about everything, but didn't love others, what good would I be? And if I had the gift of faith so that I could speak to a mountain and make it move, without love I would be no good to anybody.[3] If I gave everything I have to the poor and even sacrificed my body, I could boast about it; but if I didn't love others, I would be of no value whatsoever.[4] Love is patient and kind. Love is not jealous or boastful or proud[5] or rude. Love does not demand its own way. Love is not irritable, and it keeps no record of when it has been wronged.[6] It is never glad about injustice but rejoices whenever the truth wins out.[7] Love never gives up, never loses faith, is always hopeful, and endures through every circumstance. (1 Corinthians 13:1-7)

Choose your own motto from scripture

If you have not already done so, take a look through the scriptures (the Gospels and Psalms are an obvious source) and identify a line which impresses, inspires or challenges you. Write it down. If you have already chosen one before, does your choice still speak to you? If not, seek out another one.

You must shine in the world like bright stars, because you are offering it the word of life. (Philippians 2:15-16)

Be-attitudes for the Catholic teacher

I have called you by your name, you are mine. (Isaiah 43:2)

Identify moments when you have had a clear awareness of God's presence in your life. How did this feel? How did you respond?

You have the message of eternal life, and we believe. (John 6:68-69)

Are you deepening and updating your understanding of theology and Church teaching? The Truth is a person: are you developing your relationship with Jesus our Truth?

I will celebrate your love for ever. (Psalm 89:1)

How fully are you participating in the liturgy? Are you offering your gifts in the service of your community?
Do you make time for private prayer?

Your faith has made you whole. (Mark 5:34)

Our relationship with Jesus should make us witnesses of his love: does our faith inform every aspect of our lives or are there areas which are 'off-limits' to God? Are you living a joined-up-life?

Be of good courage; I have overcome the world. (John 16:33)

People will often deride or dismiss our faith: how do we react? Do we persevere or run for cover in silence?

I will love Unloved. (Hosea 2:23)

Who are the Unloved in our midst? Whom do *we* consign to the category of Unloved?

MONTHLY REFLECTION CALENDARS

An Overview

The basic structure of these reflections is designed to develop five strengths or competencies we look for in a Catholic teacher:

- to grow more familiar with scripture and acquire the habit of praying with the Gospels
- to experience something of the Church's devotional life
- to see the Liturgy as a place where faith, teaching and life come together
- to deepen their understanding of the Church's teaching and know where to look for answers
- to develop their own spiritual vocabulary by recording their own response to these reflections.

In the following pages you will find a *sample* of the kind of reflections we use in our programme. There are four calendars to cover four years of a university programme. Obviously the format differs slightly from the one used by students; for example, the student version is 'a month to a page' and contains a sizeable section for the personal comment referred to above.

A conscious effort is made to refer to the relevant sections of the *Alive-O* programme used in Primary schools. Reflection Calendar I is aimed at all teachers, both Primary and Secondary.

I would like us to reflect on some 'Catholic' words: although none of these are exclusive to the Catholic tradition, they do hold a special place in the spiritual vocabulary of Catholics. The aim of this exercise is to help you 'brush up' on this language but also to invite reflection on how *meaningful* these ideas are in your own life.

September – Presence

> See, I am with you always, to the end of time.
> (Matthew 28:20)

1 This is a key promise which Jesus makes to the Church and to each one of us. In what ways do you understand Jesus to be present in our world and the Church?

2 Sometimes our pupils respond to the Register or roll-call by saying 'Present' or 'Here'. Occasionally what follows during the lesson suggests that they are anything but present. It is possible to be physically present but a million miles away in terms of your own distractions and preoccupations. Be conscious of the fact that just because someone is physically with you does not necessarily mean they are *with* you!

3 If you excuse the pun, *presence is a gift*: being with others is a way of affirming them, consoling them, reassuring them. Some people have the even rarer gift of making the person they are talking to feel like the only person in the world: I think Jesus has that gift. Can you find examples from the Gospels?

October – Reverence

> As Jesus was starting on his way again, a man ran up, knelt before him, and asked him, 'Good Teacher, what must I do to receive eternal life?' (Mark 10:17)

1 This is one of several instances in the Gospel where people approach Jesus and *kneel* before him. Kneeling is one of a variety of gestures by which we express reverence for people. The Catholic tradition makes use of posture and body language to convey respect for God, the Blessed Sacrament etc. What other ways do we show respect?

2 It is important that gestures of reverence actually express what is going on inside us – or else they become devoid of meaning (the kiss of Judas in Gethsemane is literally 'lip-service'). Do you take the Sacred for granted?

3 How can you express reverence for your students and colleagues? Is this different from courtesy?

November – Remembering

> Then he took the bread, said the blessing, broke it, and gave it to them, saying, 'This is my body, which will be given for you; do this in memory of me. (Luke 22:19)

1 There is a special kind of memory which makes the past alive and real in the present: this is the kind of memory Jesus is speaking about at the Last Supper. We are asked to cultivate an attitude of 'holy remembering'. Why? How does this memory help us?

2 During this month we are invited to remember the names and lives of our departed brothers and sisters: this is always a healthy exercise.

3 Some memories are not so life-giving: do you experience 'unholy remembering', where pain or guilt from the past invade the present moment? Ask God to help you cast these wounds into 'the sea of forgetfulness' (Micah 7:19).

December / January – Gifts

1 At this time our thoughts tend to the giving and receiving of gifts. St Paul reminds us that the most important gifts (in Greek, *charismata*) are not so much material as spiritual. In case you have not done this for a while – if at all – make a list of the gifts you have. And check it twice!
2 Not for us the storing of unopened, unused gifts: if you are not using it, you *will* be losing it. By the same token, using what you are given for the good of others leads to growth.
3 Do you understand the symbolism of the gifts of gold, frankincense and myrrh? Some personal research might yield some interesting discoveries for you.

February – Thanksgiving

> Always be thankful. Let the message of Christ, in all its richness, find a home with you. (Colossians 3:15-16)

1 If there is one key attitude which distinguishes the Christian it is thankfulness. The prayer of Jesus is basically one of praise and thanks to his Father, leading up to its highest expression in the Last Supper. Remember that the word 'Eucharist' itself means 'thanksgiving'.
2 As well as giving thanks at the first Eucharist, Jesus also gives himself. In a sense *saying* 'thanks' is only half the story. Grateful people are also graceful people: in return for what they have been given they make a gift of themselves.

> With all your heart honour your father, never forget the birth-pangs of your mother. Remember that you owe your birth to them; how can you repay them for what they have done for you. (Ecclesiasticus 7:27-28)

3 Among the tasks set before us as educators must surely be the cultivation of a thankful spirit in our young people. What factors in modern life militate against such a spirit?

March – Repentance and Conversion

These words are so closely linked it is a pity to separate them. Perhaps they should be joined by 'n' (like *salt 'n' vinegar*)? Both terms shed light on two sides of the one process. First, there is a dissatisfaction that flows into regret and sorrow about the direction of one's life. Second, there is a positive desire to change that direction – even if it involves an about-turn. Sometimes, however, we get stalled at the first stage and end up wallowing in a kind of loathing of *where* we are and *who* we are. Be very wary of getting stuck.

The Season of Lent begins for many people with the injunction 'repent and believe the Gospel'. What might look like a throwaway phrase is actually quite a profound challenge. Firstly, we often have a familiarity with the Gospel but live as though it does not really impinge on our lives. Secondly, the Church proposes acceptance of the Gospel as a way of getting 'unstuck' from that first stage of sorrow and dissatisfaction. The Gospel becomes a compass for new paths.

Repentance and conversion are not simply about changing. It may be that we are so distracted and pulled in *different* and *opposing* directions that 'R'n'C' is actually about making the most of where we find ourselves. While calling on the crowds to repent and change themselves, John the Baptist also berates those who fail to make the most of what they have going for them (Luke 3:10-14).

April – Witness

> You will stand before governors and kings for my
> sake, to bear witness before them ... (Mark 13:9)

All authentic witness is about being faithful to the truth and, for the Christian, that truth is a person. We can sometimes allow ourselves to become disconnected from the true purpose of bearing witness when we lose sight of Christ: it is for *his* sake.

Genuine witness costs. Our word 'martyr' comes from the Greek word for witness. The martyrs bore witness to Christ in laying down their lives for his sake and for the encouragement of others. Quite apart from the amphitheatres of Rome and the killing fields of recent history, there are different arenas of witness. Where and how are you called to witness? How does this cost you?

May – Holiness

> Be holy, as your heavenly Father is holy.
> (Matthew 5:48)

One of the central planks of the Second Vatican Council was the universal call to holiness. *Everyone*, no matter their state of life, is called to reflect God's holiness. Taken at face value, however, those words of Jesus can be a little daunting. Note, however, that Our Lord is not telling us to be *as* holy as God – since that would be impossible. What Jesus *is* saying is that holiness should be our truest nature, our family resemblance.

Remember the link between *holiness* and *wholeness*: this goes beyond the similar sounds we make when saying them.

This Roman graffito dates from between 150 and 250 AD and is satirising the faith of a young Christian, Alexamenos. Alexamenos' god is a crucified figure with the head of a donkey. Ridicule is not a recent addition to the armoury of persecution. Expect some yourself.

A radically healthy person should also have a well-developed spiritual life. That is not to say, however, that those who suffer in mind or body are somehow deficient in holiness – quite the opposite. Many of the great saints have suffered from physical, emotional or even psychological difficulties. What connects holiness and wholeness is the idea of integrity: God's grace helps us to live with all those bits of our nature in a kind of balance. Each aspect supports and enriches the others. This is partly why the Church makes such an effort to present the mystery of the Holy Trinity to us: God's holiness is a model of communion and integrity.

June – Beauty

> You are the fairest of the children of men and graciousness is poured upon your lips. (Psalm 44)

To say that 'beauty is only skin deep' is only half true: we should not overlook the beauty that emanates from within and shows itself in noble words and loving actions. Our thirst for beauty is deep-rooted. As a race we seek out beauty and try to represent it. The rich tradition of Christian art and architecture is a reflection of this. Be aware of your senses as windows to transcendence. Would you feel comfortable 'bearing witness' to others about the things you find beautiful?

MONTHLY REFLECTION CALENDAR II

September

By the end of this month you should …

1 Prayerfully read Matthew 18:1-5.10 ('Their angels in heaven are continually in the presence of my Father'), which is the Gospel for the Feast of the Guardian Angels that is celebrated on 2 October each year. (I know this is September!) Read also paragraphs 328–336 of the *Catechism of the Catholic Church*.

Angels are important figures in the Scriptures and throughout Christian tradition (as well as in other religious traditions), yet many people feel uncomfortable with the idea of angels. Some feel that we have 'outgrown' the guardian angels. Angels are, however, included in the Creed among 'all that is seen and unseen' and the Church's teaching and liturgy makes many references to them.

October

By the end of this month you should …

1 Prayerfully read Romans 12:3-21 ('Let your love be genuine'). This is St Paul's 'lesson plan' for life. Make it yours. Write down any phrase that strikes you.

2 October is the month of the Rosary. *Alive-O 7* has a series of lessons on 'Mary and the Mysteries of Light'. Take some time to read through the background notes and the lesson plans.

3 Children enjoy dressing up for Hallowe'en ('the eve of All Hallows' or All Saints day) but some people feel

uncomfortable with its pagan associations. Could you suggest ways of celebrating Hallowe'en with your class? (*Alive-O 2* has some suggestions.)

November

By the end of this month you should ...

1 Prayerfully read Matthew 5:1-12 ('Rejoice and be glad for your reward will be great in heaven'), which is the Gospel for the feast of All Saints. In this Gospel we hear Jesus preaching the Sermon on the Mount. Can you think of people you know who fit the description of the blessed? Don't just think of saints or famous people but of people you know – perhaps family members.

2 In November we celebrate the feasts of Scotland's patron saints: St Margaret (16 November) and St Andrew (30 November). Find out more about these saints. (Although it's a term 3 lesson, *Alive-O 6* has some material on St Margaret; *Alive-O 7* also has some material on saints in term 1.) It is important that teachers are aware of their own national celebration.

3 Enrol the names of deceased family members in the book of remembrance in your parish or here in the department.

December

By the end of this month you should ...

1 Prayerfully read Matthew 1:1-25 ('The ancestry of Jesus Christ, the son of David'), which is the Gospel for the Vigil Mass of Christmas. It is not easy to read this passage prayerfully! Although it begins with a long list of unfamiliar-sounding names, it is important to remember that Jesus is born into a family like everyone else. Among those named are people who did terrible things, as well as those who did wonderful things. God chose to be born into a family with quite a few 'black sheep'! As we draw close to the family season of Christmas, pray for your own family.

2 More parishes are making use of the Jesse tree in their Advent preparations. Find out more about it.
3 Think about celebrating the sacrament of Reconciliation as part of your Christmas preparations.

January

By the end of this month you should ...

1 Prayerfully read 2 Timothy 1:1-8 ('I am reminded of the sincere faith which you have'), which is the first reading for the feast of St Timothy on 26 January. Timothy was a young helper of St Paul. Look at the language St Paul uses to encourage this young teacher. Notice also the role played by family in passing on the faith (faith is 'caught' not 'taught').
2 The conversion of St Paul is also celebrated this month (25 January). Paul is often referred to as 'the apostle of the nations' and his missionary journeys spanned most of the known world. He very clearly taught that everyone is called to holiness. Read paragraphs 2566–2567 of the Catechism of the Catholic Church to see what it says about this call to holiness.
3 St Paul shares his feast day with Robert Burns! Perhaps you could teach your class the Selkirk grace:

> Some hae meat and cannot eat.
> Some cannot eat that want it:
> But we hae meat and we can eat,
> Sae let the Lord be thankit.

You will need to translate it for them! Do you pray before or after meals?

February

By the end of this month you should ...

1 Prayerfully read 1 Corinthians 12:31-13:13 ('There are three things that last: faith, hope and love, and the

greatest of these is love'), which is a favourite at weddings!

2 This passage contains a very helpful examination of conscience. Whenever it says 'love', put your own name (for example, 'John is always patient and kind') and see how true that statement is. We explain sin to children as a failure to show love, so this reflection helps us to see just how loving we really are.

3 How does the *Catechism of the Catholic Church* define sin (paragraphs 1849–1851)?

4 Make sure you are familiar with the prayers used in *Alive-O* for confession: the prayer for forgiveness, the Confiteor, the act of sorrow and the prayer after forgiveness.

March

By the end of this month you should ...

1 Prayerfully read Luke 1:26-38 ('You are to conceive and bear a son'), which is the Gospel for the feast of the Annunciation. This is where Mary's vocation is made clear to her for the first time. Notice how she reacts at first. How would you react?

2 The Church teaches that every one of us is unique and 'unrepeatable': no one else can do exactly what I am called to do with my life. Each of us has a personal vocation that seldom emerges suddenly like the Gospel story. Usually our vocation gradually dawns on us but, once we realise what it is, we could not imagine 'being' anything else. Presumably you are studying this course because you feel God is calling you to be a teacher. Remember that this is a spiritual calling as well as a job.

3 Read this prayer:

> Teacher's Prayer
> I want to teach my students how to live this life
> on earth, to face its struggles and its strife

and improve their worth.
Not just the lesson in a book or how the rivers
flow, but how to choose the proper path
wherever they may go.
To understand eternal truth and know the right
from wrong and gather all the beauty of a
flower and a song.
For if I help the world to grow in wisdom and
grace
then I shall feel that I have won and I have filled
my place.
And so I ask your guidance, God
that I may do my part for character and
confidence
and happiness of heart.
Amen.

April

By the end of this month you should ...

1 Prayerfully read John 21:15-19 ('Feed my lambs, feed my sheep'). Jesus comes to his disciples after his resurrection and makes time for Peter. Jesus asks Peter, 'Do you love me?' three times. Some scholars see this as his way of helping Peter 'undo' the three denials of Jesus after his arrest. It is also Christ's way of handing on his role as shepherd to Peter. In fact Jesus himself is acting as Peter's shepherd.

2 Our word 'pastoral' comes from the word 'pastor' or 'shepherd'. How clearly do you understand your own pastoral role?

May

By the end of this month you should ...

1 Prayerfully read Genesis 1:26-2:3 ('Fill the earth and conquer it'), which is the first reading for the Feast of St

Joseph the Worker on 1 May. It describes God's work in creating the universe but also emphasises the importance of rest. (Remember this is not meant to be a literal account of how the world came about! It does, however, convey the truth about work as creative and the need for recreation.) We work to live – not the other way about!

2 The Church has a rich body of social teaching. Why not visit the website of the Holy See (www.vatican.va) to explore some of these often overlooked teachings?

3 This is a month of special devotion to Our Lady. Explore some ways of marking this with a class.

4 Look at the teacher's notes in *Alive-O 7* about 'Teaching the Senior-Primary Schoolchild to Pray' (pp. 21–24). This will also give you some insights into prayer in general.

June

By the end of this month you should …

1 Prayerfully read John 12:24-26 ('If a grain of wheat dies, it yields a rich harvest'). This is a Gospel that is often associated with martyrs. What stands out for you in this passage?

2 The word 'martyr' means 'witness' and in the Christian sense it refers to someone who is prepared to surrender life rather than surrender Jesus. It does not mean someone who takes their own life and the lives of others. Did you know that more Christian martyrs died in the twentieth century than the other nineteen put together?

3 Find out more about one of these contemporary martyrs. An internet search will provide you with much information. Here are some suggestions: Gianna Molla, Jerzy Popieluszko, Ceferino Jiménez Malla. Each is a different kind of martyr, but what common bond do they share?

September

By the end of this month you should ...

1 Prayerfully read St Paul's letter to the Philippians 2:6-11 ('Jesus humbled himself, therefore God raised him high'), which is the second reading for the Feast of the Triumph of the Cross on 14 September. There is a strong message about Christ's humility.

2 Did you know that this feast gives its name to the Scottish Parliament which is based at Holyrood in Edinburgh? 'Holy Rood' is the old English for 'Holy Cross'.

3 The early Christians were ashamed of the cross (they inherited the Jewish view that 'to hang upon the tree was a sign of God's curse') and the cross was not represented in art until the year 430 AD. Compare that with the situation today when many people wear crucifixes as accessories without much understanding of their symbolism. How would you speak to a class about the importance of the cross?

October

By the end of this month you should ...

1 Prayerfully read Matthew 6:28 ('Consider the lilies of the field'). Jesus refers constantly to the beauty of the natural world. During this month we begin to see a clear change as autumn begins to change the colours around us. Make an effort to walk in the park! Look at the beauty of trees, leaves etc.

2 St Francis of Assisi is often regarded as the 'saint of the environment'. Find out more about him (*Alive-O 6* has a week dedicated to him) and his 'Canticle of Creation'.

3 The Church also has a 'green' message. Look at paragraphs of the Catechism which outline the Church's teaching on the environment.

4 October is also the month of the Rosary: look at the mysteries of the Rosary once again (all twenty of them!). What are the advantages of this kind of prayer?

November

By the end of this month you should …
1 Prayerfully read Hebrews 12:1-2 ('With so many witnesses in a great cloud on every side of us …').
2 This month begins with the Feast of All Saints. Why do you think we pray to the saints? If you haven't spoken to your Confirmation saint for a while, perhaps this month would be a good time to do so.
3 Look at what the Catechism says about 'the Communion of saints'.
4 Read the Apostles' Creed. Make sure you have a copy in your R.E. file.

December

By the end of this month you should …
1 Prayerfully read Matthew 1:18-25 ('Mary will give birth to a son and you will name him Jesus'). This is the Gospel from the Vigil Mass at Christmas. Put yourself in Joseph's position. Ask yourself the following questions: how would you have reacted when you discovered that Mary was 'found to be with child'? (Remember that, unlike the Christmas card picture we have of St Joseph, he was probably not far out of his teens.) What would have been the consequences of the 'publicity' around Mary?
2 Find out more about the origins of the crib scene. An internet search should help you find out more about St Francis and the crib at Greccio.
3 Encourage your class to send Christmas cards which show the Christmas message or support a good cause.

January

By the end of this month you should ...

1 Prayerfully read Matthew 2:1-12 ('We saw his star and came to do him homage'), which is the Gospel for the Feast of the Epiphany. Where would you look for a king? Reflect on what this Gospel tells us about being truly 'wise'.

2 There is a strong connection between the Advent themes of darkness and light and this Feast of the Epiphany. Look at the lessons 'The People who Walked in Darkness' through to 'Returning – A New Beginning' in *Alive-O 4*. See how these connections are made and brought out into the light.

3 Find out more about the way this feast is celebrated by Eastern Christians (today is really their 'Christmas' day). An internet search might help!

4 Be sure you know the carol 'We three kings'. Note that the Gospel does not call the wise men 'kings' at all!

February

By the end of this month you should ...

1 Prayerfully read Luke 2:22-40 ('My eyes have seen your salvation'), which is the Gospel of the Feast of the Presentation on 2 February. Notice the respect that is given to the two old people in the Temple. This Gospel is about promises fulfilled. God is always faithful, always to be trusted. Ask for greater trust in your own life.

2 The Feast of the Presentation is also called 'Candlemas' and is celebrated forty days after Christmas. Traditionally the candles which were to be used for the rest of the year were blessed on this day. What do candles symbolise for people? Why are candles symbols of prayer?

3 This feast has two meanings. It celebrates the presentation of Jesus in the Temple according to the Law of Moses. It also used to be called the feast of the 'purification' of

Mary since the same Law held that women who had given birth had to undergo 'purification'. Read this short poem by John Boyd, SJ, and reflect on what it says about Mary. Look at the way she is compared to a candle.

Candlemas
Beewise we gather our wax all year
from bramble sorrow and thistle tear, Briar
sadness and spine of pain:
bitter flowers that bloom again! But deadest
winter brings a day
when thorns have lovelier bloom than May;
When candles are fashioned and lit by One who
fashioned her wax to be lit by the Sun, Then
watched her Candle burn: the price
of sin-consuming sacrifice. Today she shares the
Flame anew
to make us priest-and-victim too.
and Mary-mothered flames and Flame
live their sacrificial Name.

March
By the end of this month you should ...

1 Prayerfully read Matthew 6:1-18 ('Your Father, who sees all that is done in secret, will reward you'), which is the Gospel for Ash Wednesday. How hard is it to get the balance right between what we show on the 'outside' and what is happening on the 'inside'? Do you feel pressure to be superficial in your dealings with others and the kind of judgements you make?

2 Find out what resources SCIAF (Scottish Catholic International Aid Fund; partner of Trócaire, CAFOD, etc.) has made available for Lent this year. What is your class / school doing to help others this Lent?

3 Although Ash Wednesday was last month, make sure you

know about where ashes come from and why we wear ashes at the beginning of the season of Lent.

April

By the end of this month you should ...

1 Prayerfully read Luke 24:1-12 ('Why look among the dead for someone who is alive?'), which a Gospel for the Easter Vigil. Notice how women were the first people to hear about the Resurrection of Jesus. Notice also the reaction of the apostles to the news! Is there a phrase in this passage that particularly strikes you as summing up the Easter message? Write it down; remember it.

2 Read paragraphs of the *Catechism of the Catholic Church* about the Resurrection of Jesus. Why is the physical (bodily) Resurrection of Jesus so important to Christians?

3 Look at *Alive-O 7* and the teachers' notes for the lesson 'Easter – The Risen Jesus is present at Mass'. Read the advice it gives for planning a class Mass.

May

By the end of this month you should ...

1 Prayerfully read Acts 2:1-11 ('They were all filled with the Holy Spirit and began to speak'), which is the first reading for the Solemnity of Pentecost. What do you find the most striking aspect of this account? Look at the symbols that are used to describe the Holy Spirit's presence: which of the seven sacraments does this suggest to you?

2 Find a Sacramentary or Missal and look up the Preface for Pentecost (the preface is the prayer which begins 'The Lord be with you ... Lift up your hearts' etc.). This is a good summary of Pentecost. (Photo)copy it for your teaching file.

3 Pentecost is also when we celebrate the birthday of the Church. How would you involve a class in celebrating this occasion?

4 Remind yourself of the seven gifts of the Holy Spirit.

5 Perhaps you could pray the Glorious mysteries of the Rosary (as they include Pentecost and May is also a month of devotion to Mary).

June

By the end of this month you should ...

1 Prayerfully read Mark 14:12-16, 22-26 ('This is my body. This is my blood'), which is the Gospel for the Feast of the Body and Blood of Christ. Which phrases of this Gospel stand out for you? Although we know the words so well, we shouldn't allow ourselves to get used to the tremendous significance of what Jesus is saying.

2 Read the *Catechism of the Catholic Church* paragraphs 1373–1381 and note what it says about Jesus' presence in the Eucharist.

3 Jesus celebrated his last supper as a Passover meal. Make sure you know something about the Passover.

Passover is celebrated around the time Christians celebrate Easter. How could Easter be described as the Christian Passover? Try to think in terms of slavery / freedom, darkness / light, death / life. What do we mean by referring to Jesus as the Paschal or Passover Lamb?

September

By the end of this month you should ...

1 Prayerfully read Luke 19:1-10 (the story of Zacchaeus) with its message that Jesus came to seek and find those who were lost. What do you think prompted the turnaround in Zacchaeus' life? Have you ever met someone who 'lived down' to other people's expectations but 'blossomed' when given the chance? Be aware that this is often true of children who present challenging behaviour.

2 Some people feel lost and cut adrift from the Church. September is often the month when parishes invite people who have questions about the faith, either because they are interested in becoming Catholics or because they have lapsed from the practice of the faith, to come forward. Many parents you will meet will not have an active connection with the parish. You may be the person who helps bring them back into a relationship with the Church. This is a truly Christ-like dimension of teaching.

October

By the end of this month you should ...

1 Complete your own personal formation statement.

2 Prayerfully read Matthew 18:1-5 ('Unless you become like little children you will never enter the Kingdom of Heaven') and reflect on its message for you.

3 As this is the month of the Rosary, re-acquaint yourself with the Mysteries of the Rosary (including the new Mysteries of Light).

4 How would you prepare a lesson on the Rosary for Primary 5/3rd Class?

November

By the end of this month you should ...

1 Prayerfully read Luke 7:11-17 about Jesus bringing a young man back to life.
2 Ask yourself the following questions:
   - What do you think the boy said at the moment he came back to life?
   - What did he experience?
   - What did Jesus say?
   - What does this passage mean to you?
3 Look over what the *Catechism of the Catholic Church* says about death and the afterlife (paragraphs 1020–1050).
4 Teach your class (or yourself!) the prayer 'Eternal rest grant unto them'.
5 How would you talk to your class about remembering and praying for the faithful departed?

December

By the end of this month you should ...

1 Prayerfully read Isaiah 9:1-7 ('A son is given to us'). This is the first reading at Midnight Mass. The figure of a child is used to bring in a new age of peace and justice. What words or phrases really strike you? Pray for peace in our world as you prepare for Christmas.
2 Alongside your chocolate Advent calendar, make sure you have a religious one. Think about writing down a line from scripture each day of Advent.
3 Plan a carol service for your class. What readings would you use? Think about writing a short reflection on each of the 'stars' of the Nativity story.
4 Advent is a time of preparation. How are your spiritual preparations going?

January

By the end of this month you should ...

1 Prayerfully read Mark 1:7-11 which is the account of Jesus' baptism. What strikes you about this account in Mark's Gospel? John trying to talk Jesus out of it? Perhaps Jesus insisting on it? Why do you think Jesus wants to be baptised? (Remember that he does not need baptism as we do.)

2 Look over what the *Catechism of the Catholic Church* says about baptism (paragraphs 1213–1274).

3 Think about how you might talk to your class about baptism. Look at the *Alive-O* materials. You might consider using other 'hands on' activities to show the importance of water, light and oil. Can you think of ways of helping children 're-live' their own baptism?

4 Familiarise yourself with the text of the Promises and the Profession of Faith used at baptism (it is also used at Confirmation, remember).

February

By the end of this month you should ...

1 Prayerfully read Matthew 4:1-11 ('Jesus fasts for forty days and is tempted'). Look at how the devil tries to throw Jesus off course: what temptations does he use? The devil begins his temptations with the word 'if', as if trying to get Jesus to doubt who he is and pull off a 'stunt' to prove it. So many temptations in our lives arise when we doubt or forget who we are. Ask God to show you where temptations occur in your own life.

2 Read what the Catechism says about Satan tempting Jesus (paragraphs 538–540) and temptation in general (2846–2849).

3 Prepare a class for the Sacrament of Reconciliation or Confession. How would you help a class examine their

conscience? Make sure you know the Act(s) of Contrition used in your local sacramental programme.

March

By the end of this month you should ...

1 Prayerfully read John 13:1-15 ('Now he showed how perfect his love was') where Jesus washes the feet of his disciples. Imagine what that scene was like. Be present. Look at the reaction of the apostles. Why did Peter react in that way? John's Gospel has no account of the last supper (or the first Mass), only this story. What do you think John is saying about the meaning of the Eucharist?

2 Find and use, *or write your own* Stations of the Cross for Children (there are plenty of examples available). Try to understand how the Stations of the Cross came about. Make sure you know the prayer at the beginning and end of each station.

3 Lent is a time for works of charity as well as self-denial. How would you explain this to a class of primary school children?

April

By the end of this month you should ...

1 Prayerfully read John 20:19-31, which describes Jesus' first appearance to his disciples after his Resurrection. Thomas is not there, but imagine *you* are: how would you feel at seeing Jesus again? Would you be anxious about what he would say knowing that you ran away? Look at how Jesus treats his disciples. Why do you think Thomas reacts in the way he does? What would you do in his position? Why do you think Jesus still has wounds (in other stories of his appearances after Easter, he has no wounds)?

2 Find a missal or sacramentary and read the Church's Easter proclamation at the Easter Vigil. (It begins

'Rejoice heavenly powers!') This is a summary of what Easter means to the Church as a whole and each one of us individually. Write down any phrases that particularly strike you.

May

By the end of this month you should ...

1 Prayerfully read Luke 1:39-56 ('The Almighty has done great things for me, he has exalted the lowly'). Try to take the place of either Mary or Elizabeth and imagine what your own 'news' means to the other. Perhaps you could write your own 'song of joy' for all the good things and people in your life and invite your class to do the same.

2 Make sure you are comfortable with the Marian prayers: Hail Mary, the *Memorare* ('Remember, O most gracious virgin Mary'), the 'Hail Holy Queen' and the Angelus. (All are included in *Alive-O*.)

June

By the end of this month you should ...

1 Prayerfully read Hosea 11:1.3-4.8-9 ('I lead them with reins of kindness, with leading strings of love'). Look at the imagery used here. What does this language tell you about God's love for us and you? 'They have not understood that I was the one looking after them': reflect on that phrase in your own life and the lives of the people you love.

2 Try to learn something about devotion to the Sacred Heart and how it can be made meaningful for you. (Many schools still come to Mass on the 'First Friday' of the month. Make sure you understand why devotions like this are still important.)

THE LIGHT OF HIS FACE

ADVENT REFLECTIONS

My eldest niece and her husband are expecting their first child in the spring of next year. I asked them to give me some words which described how they feel, both as individuals and as a couple. As I looked at the list, I was struck by the way in which they reflected what must have been going on in the lives of Mary and Joseph. I think they also have something to say to each of us about our lives. I invite you to take a few moments each day (well, from 1 December anyway!) to consider these ...

Amazed

It is an amazing thing to hear that you are going to have a baby. Amazement can be a mix of wonder and disbelief: look at how Mary reacted to the angel's message. Amazement need not be a fleeting thing. We have many amazing people and things in our lives. Name them (in your heart if not 'out loud'!).

Alive

To have a child growing inside you is to be doubly alive. Saint Irenaeus tells us that 'the glory of God is man fully alive'. Think about what makes you feel most intensely alive: do you share those moments with God?

Fragile

An expectant mother can sometimes feel very fragile. Some things are 'off the menu', some activities must be foregone for the sake of the baby. All of us can feel fragile at times. It can be that the more *alive* we feel, the more we realise just how *slight* our grip on life is. To feel your pulse can be an exhilarating experience which affirms that you are alive; it can also be a reminder of the drumbeat of mortality. One day, no one knows when, that pulse will cease. How do you deal with your fragile moments? Do you ignore them or do you go to the other extreme?

Fruitful

God wants each one of us, no matter who we may be, to experience fruitfulness. 'I chose you,' says Jesus, 'and I commissioned you to go out and bear fruit, fruit that will last.' Do you have a sense of your gifts bearing fruit? Are you aware of the ways in which you can be creative? If not, why not?

Dizzy

An unpleasant side-effect of all this fruitfulness can be light-headedness. People can also be 'existentially dizzy' – pulled in different directions, running around without much purpose or direction – the sense of being disorientated is just as uncomfortable. Use prayer time to help you get your Advent bearings.

Cravings

Cravings are strong (sometimes irrational and uncontrollable) urges. In a sense they cannot be satisfied. Instead of being satisfied we can be left wanting more, and more. Although they appear trivial, they are really implied in the last two petitions in the Lord's Prayer: 'lead us not into temptation, but deliver us from evil'. Do you experience the pull of cravings? You may be able to name some obvious ones, but other more subtle cravings might also have a strengthening grip on you.

Changing

A pregnant woman observes many changes in her body as it grows and alters its shape to accommodate the baby. The Jews of the Old Testament had mixed feelings about pregnancy itself. They had a fear of any alteration in the body. We seem to have inherited this same fear from our ancestors: we may become less at home in our own skin as we grow older, put on weight, as we discover that our bodies may not be working as well as they should be. Most people harbour a fear of unseen growth inside their body. Christmas is about the Word becoming flesh. Real flesh, like ours. How comfortable are you in your own flesh?

Laughter

There is much happiness and laughter during the months leading up to the birth of a child (not all of it due to mood swings and hormones). Laughter is an essential ingredient of the Christian life. When did you last have a really good laugh?

Tears

As with laughter, so with tears. Tears are a fact of life. They were certainly a feature of our Lord's life. We are all touched by sadness whether it arises out of the lives of others or our own. Not everyone gives in to tears but we all need channels for expressing (and expelling) our grief. Many of the world's problems stem from misdirected anger and unresolved grief.

Thankful

New life is an occasion for thankfulness. All our lives are meant to be profoundly 'Eucharistic' ('giving thanks'). Be consciously thankful for all the blessings of your life.

Looking forward

'What will this child grow up to be?' Each one of us is 'unrepeatably unique' and we have a distinct purpose in life.

No matter what stage of our lives we may be at, we are still on this journey of becoming. Keep looking forward to today. And tomorrow.

Preparing
The season of Advent is one of real preparation. Just as a family gets ready to welcome a new child, we should be preparing our hearts as a fitting place for God's Son. Think of it as 'pre-prayering'.

Reading
Many expectant mothers spend a lot of time reading books and baby manuals to help them give birth. Perhaps we could take five minutes each day to read God's word so that we too might 'bring forth Christ' in our world.

Worrying
It is only natural to worry that everything is going to plan and that the baby is healthy. Too much worry, however, can be a health hazard to mother and baby. The same is true of life in general. If you have some worries hanging over you, make sure you share them with God (and a friend). Do not allow your worries to paralyse you!

Connecting
Sometimes carrying a baby makes a woman more aware of the bond of love with her own mother. Advent should be a time for us to reconnect with those who gave us life. Even if they have passed beyond this world, they are still joined to us in the Communion of Saints. Take time to talk to your loved ones today.

Dreaming
Dreams can be our way of tidying up and making sense of the thoughts, images and feelings we have experienced during

the day. They can also be a deep well of meanings and God can communicate with us in our dreams (just as he did with St Joseph on more than one occasion). Do not despise your dreams or dismiss them out of hand!

Sleeping

We all need to surrender to sleep in order to recharge our batteries. Is anything disturbing your rest – both physical and spiritual? Make sure you take time to rest amidst the 'busyness' of these days.

Waking

'Wake up! Shake off the night!' Make your first thought on waking the prayer, 'I will serve'.

Loving

The new life of the child is nurtured in love. The child is, in a sense, love personified. Love between two people is not a 'thing' to be consumed by them but becomes a person in its own right. It is an echo of the mystery of the Incarnation itself. Remember that YOU are also 'love made flesh'. Love is your vocation. Consciously live out that vocation today.

Comparing

An anxious mother may look at other mothers and compare herself with them. Is she smaller? Bigger? Older? Younger? We all have a tendency to compare ourselves with others and sometimes we can fool ourselves into thinking that we would be happier as someone else. This is always a mistake. We spend so much time thinking about someone else's life that we stop living our own. It is perfectly alright for us to spend some time today looking *within*.

Helping

People tend to fuss over expectant mums, getting them to put their feet up and running errands for them. Helping is serving. It is the most simple and direct way to put our baptismal calling into practice. Look for those occasions of grace, those opportunities to serve today.

Holding
Sometimes we can feel unloved or unlovable. A touch can overcome that. We have bodies for this very reason. The message of Christmas is about a God who makes himself *tangible*. Our Lord made good use of the agency of touch to console and heal those who were sick, possessed or unregarded by society. Remember that touch is potentially holy. Remember also that we can 'hold' someone in prayer by making them the focus of our thoughts and intercession.

Buying
Much of the activity surrounding a child's birth involves buying things: gifts, clothes and furniture for the 'new arrival'. Buying is also a significant part of our Christmas activities. Alongside the material things which feature on our lists, identify at least one spiritual gift you would like to give someone in your life. Pray about it.

Watching, waiting
At the end of months' waiting, Joseph, like every other father, had to stand back and wait. Sometimes watching and waiting can seem *powerless* experiences. In reality they are *powerful*: they make us realise God's power over our lives. As you count down the hours to Christmas, invite God to give you a patient, watchful heart like Joseph.

THE TEACHER'S ROSARY

Although the Rosary is easily dismissed as an outmoded form of prayer, it can, as I hope I have described earlier, offer a way of reflecting upon those bits of our human experience which we share with the protagonists of the Gospel. When other words fail us, the Rosary can offer a framework for our thoughts or perhaps even a sort of scaffolding to which we can tie our thoughts when everything else seems to be coming adrift. Although I have gathered these reflections under the heading of *The Teacher's Rosary*, they are general enough to cross over into any sphere of work or life.

Even if the prospect of praying the respective decades of 'Hail Mary's' one after the other leaves you cold, you might derive some benefit from exploring these mysteries as part of your own prayer. After all, the word 'mystery' has more to do with opening windows than solving puzzles. For example, some of these reflections could form part of an exercise in *Lectio Divina*.

The Joyful Mysteries

The Annunciation: On courtesy
The angel and the woman engage in a gracious conversation. No orders are given, but God's plan is presented as a scenario which only the most shuttered soul could refuse. The courtesy of this encounter is arresting: Gabriel's words stir life in the womb of the Virgin and she has shown herself worthy of the greeting 'highly favoured'.

How do I express my 'will'? Is it delivered as an ultimatum or an invitation? Am I aware of the power of words and my ability to build up or knock down by what I say and how I say it?

The Visitation: On cooperation

The helping hand extended to Elizabeth is itself a lesson in cooperation. Mary was not sent for but took the initiative; she comes not so much as a helper but as a sharer in joy since Elizabeth had also been touched by the grace of God who had 'taken away her shame'. Both women are cooperators with God and each other. In a very real sense what Mary does for Elizabeth is not as important as what Elizabeth does for Mary: her greeting confirms what the angel had spoken – she had indeed become the Mother of the Lord.

How ready am I to help others, especially if it makes demands which are beyond the call of duty or contract? Do I take the initiative in offering help to someone who might be slow to ask? By the same token, do I graciously accept support when it is offered to me? Remember that faith is confirmed (or strengthened) in charity.

The Nativity: On difficult births

Beneath the sentimentality which so often attends our recreations of the Nativity story lies a deeply unsentimental truth: God is born into a world of shadows in which shepherds and kings offer us glimpses into the lives of the poor and unregarded or the rich and insecure. In the midst sits Mary who contemplates the raising of the lowly and the fall of the mighty. There too lies the child who is the cause of all this: a new life already overshadowed by the threat of death.

It is important to acknowledge that all births and beginnings carry an element of risk. The risk may lie in our hopes being

THE LIGHT OF HIS FACE

too fragile or our designs too rigid. Sometimes the struggle comes from the opposition of others who, Herod-like, feel threatened by change or any initiative which is not their own.

The Presentation: On the wisdom of experience
Mary and Joseph encounter Anna and Simeon: the young meet the old in God's house and something beautiful is exchanged – not so much advice as a blessing. Of course the blessing words are also hard-edged, sharp like the sword which will pierce Mary's soul. Yet here too Mary shows herself to be a woman of reflection, pondering these words and feeling their weight.

The advice of our elders is often a mixed blessing. There can be times when 'advice' is merely criticism in thin disguise. But there are times when we should listen to the wisdom of experience, that sense of proportion one acquires simply by being around long enough. Those words of Simeon in particular prove to be a mystery to Mary but she resists the temptation to ignore a message that is hard to bear or grasp. Do I jettison what I find it hard to understand or accept?

The Finding of Jesus in the Temple: On respecting space
Mary and Joseph's reactions are refreshingly unrestrained: there is that mix of anger, relief and love which any parent would recognise. Perhaps for the first time, Jesus is behaving in a way that is marking him out as an individual in his own right. He may not quite be 'testing the limits of his freedom' as children on the cusp of adolescence tend to do, but he is certainly showing a desire to communicate his inner world to those on the outside. This is a tentative step on the journey towards selfhood and a rehearsal for the Gospel.

The sword mentioned by Simeon makes a brief appearance in this passage. But it is the 'cord' binding mother and child which is being severed at this point. Mary must accept and respect her son's need to flex his muscles and live a life which is not simply an extension of her own. Difficult, apparently thoughtless behaviour is not the end of the world and more often than not the beginning of a new one. Knowing when and how to create respectful spaces for this growth is a grace. As C. Day Lewis has expressed it: 'Selfhood begins with a walking away, and love is proved in the letting go.'

The Mysteries of Light

The Baptism of Christ: On joining the queue
Christ's baptism is not like any other; he does not actually need baptism (since he is the sinless Lamb of God). So how are we to account for his appearance at the Jordan? On the one hand, his immersion in the waters of the river is a sanctifying gesture, one echoed in the celebrant lowering the Paschal candle into the font at the Easter Vigil. The Lord's baptism is also a gesture of radical humility which makes explicit God's decision to make his dwelling among us. Jesus waits his turn among sinful humanity and allows himself to be ministered to by John.

What defines a really good teacher is not only the ability to stand before a class and teach but also the courage to stand among them and share something of their lives. This is exactly what we observe in Christ our Teacher.

The Wedding at Cana: On asking for what you need
The first of the 'signs' worked by Jesus arise from two things: a simple need and a compassionate intervention. A young couple are spared the embarrassment of a wedding without wine by Mary's decision to ask her son to help. What looks at first like reluctance becomes an action of superabundant generosity.

Sometimes we know what we need but cannot quite find the words to ask for it, whether it be pride or awkwardness which hampers us. If we know someone else is in need, do we know how to intervene discreetly? If we are in a position to help, can we do that without drawing attention to ourselves or the need itself?

The Preaching of the Kingdom: On teaching as kerygma
The core of the Gospel is Christ's proclamation that the Kingdom is near at hand. He, in fact, embodied this Kingdom he was proclaiming. This message is underpinned by the miracles and healings of Christ's public ministry and continued in the preaching of the Apostles after the resurrection.

What the crowds heard from the lips of Jesus and the disciples is essentially what we proclaim to our children. This proclamation (kerygma) is the key truth at the heart of all Christian education, namely that the Christ-event changes the way we understand our world and ourselves. Far from being a marginal extra in a busy curriculum, it is the law which underpins all our reasoning and creativity.

The Transfiguration: On seeing through the eyes of love
The disciples are allowed a brief glimpse of Jesus as the Father sees him, as 'Light from Light' or even 'Love from Love'. Jesus is shown in context, between the Law and the Prophets, for that privileged audience of apostles.

Cynics and Romantics both claim that 'Love is blind'. In this mystery, however, we are shown that Grace lends a real depth to our perception. In a world where judgements both snap and superficial tend to predominate, the Transfiguration challenges us to see into the heart of people and situations.

The Institution of the Eucharist: On the sharing of life
What is about to unfold in the 'real world' is sacramentally enacted in the Last Supper with the handing over, the breaking, the pouring out. The Church reads the Passion narrative in the light of the Eucharist and understands the Mass as the death and resurrection of Jesus made real and present once again.

The Eucharist not only makes the Church, it makes the Christian too. Those gestures of blessing, breaking and sharing are written into rhythms of every Christian life and the challenge is to accept them in the same spirit of 'free acceptance' as Jesus. This is no mean feat: while we might find it easy to accept a blessing, the inevitable demands of being shared among the many can be such that we wish the cup to pass us by.

The Sorrowful Mysteries

The Agony in the Garden: On being alone with our decisions
The account of Christ's agony in Gethsemane is reminiscent in many ways of his temptation in the wilderness. Both are times of trial when, explicitly or implicitly, the temptation to be someone else is set before Jesus. Surrendering to the Devil's suggestions or running from the 'hour' would be inauthentic choices. In order to truly be himself, Jesus must see things through to the end.

Although we can be guided (or tempted) by the advice of others, most of the crucial decisions we must make in life are ours and ours alone. Before all his significant choices Jesus spends time in intense prayer and, in the examples we have just mentioned, the struggle of decision is followed by an experience of consolation. A sense of peace accompanies all genuine discernment.

The Scourging at the Pillar: On humiliation

The Roman custom of flogging condemned criminals was the overture to an appalling spectacle of torture. Whoever devised the stages of a crucifixion clearly had an understanding of how the mind works as well as the body. For not only was it a particularly cruel form of physical torment, but it was also calculated to shame the dying man by exposing his crime and his nakedness.

To be humiliated, either by another person or simply by circumstances, is a deeply wounding experience. While a physical injury may heal and fade, a mark of shame can linger on. Whenever our shortcomings or inconsistencies are exposed to the scrutiny of others, we are often surprised at how vulnerable we really are. To be deliberately humiliated or to knowingly humiliate another is an act of violence: the very expression 'a tongue lashing' says it all.

The Crowning with Thorns: On the ambiguity of success

When Jesus is crowned with a crown or 'cap' of thorns, it is part of that same routine of humiliation. The eyes of faith, however, are invited to see this as the soldiers prophesying in spite of themselves: Jesus really is a King, really is their King. This surrender to death is the crowning achievement of his life.

The cross does not look like success. What we now regard as the defining symbol of the Christian faith was, for hundreds of years, a concept which caused awkwardness and apologetic stammering. At its heart, the cross is a sign of ambiguity and revolution. The passion of Jesus is revolutionary because it upsets the 'normal' pattern of life and death. It is ambiguous because it makes us reassess what we understand by failure and victory.

The Carrying of the Cross: On emerging from the crowd
Jesus is made to carry his cross and we are invited to reflect upon this fresh misery. But this mystery also calls to mind the (admittedly forced) help given by Simon. A reluctant and potentially anonymous figure is changed by this encounter into someone whose name and family would be familiar to the young Church.

A strategy for survival (and even success) is to keep your head down, to say nothing and stand well back from the action. This was certainly not the case for Simon: although the choice was made for him by the guards he still had the option of sinking back into the crowd once he had served his purpose. Jesus was a dangerous man to know, even in death. Am I prepared to step out from the crowd to challenge an injustice or indeed to forsake the 'crowd position' altogether in order to assume a prophetic stance on life?

The Crucifixion: On confronting death
Any death is an absurdity: to see any person in death whom we have known in life is a shock to the system. The rapid and brutal transition from death to life we witness at the crucifixion is an even more unsettling contrast since it is the dux vitae, *the Lord of Life, who is dead.*

We are less and less accustomed to being around the dead. A little of that discomfort can even extend to those who mourn – we struggle to find ways of being with them and often feel tempted to absent ourselves from their presence until we can safely join the company of others. Death raises questions for us all and we should not downplay how much havoc it causes in our lives. It is especially important to be attentive to death's impact on children and young people not just in the immediate wake of bereavement but months down the line.

The Glorious Mysteries

The Resurrection: On the triumph of life

On Easter morning the Church sings of the struggle between Death and Life in which Christ though 'slain, yet lives to reign'. Of course it is not only Christ who is raised: the shock of Easter brings life to the flat-lining Apostles. The Liturgy describes them as 'men on the verge of losing hope' but this seems an altogether optimistic appraisal of the state of their hearts and minds.

Although 'Love' is the quality which strikes the loudest chord in the human heart and 'Faith' seems inextricably bound up with the word 'Christian', 'Hope' is the Easter virtue. *Surrexit spes mea*, intones the Church in that same Easter song, 'Christ, my hope, is risen'. Hope defines the Christian experience and gives it a shape when the other theological virtues seem to be but words. In the bleakest, sealed-tomb moments in life, the Paschal Mystery must refresh those corners of our hearts which despair of the sun rising and a new day.

The Ascension: On moving on

The forty days after Easter must surely be the most emotionally turbulent in human history – from the abject despair of the cross to the joy of Easter to the strange parting on the hillside outside Jerusalem – all human life is here. The apostles are jolted from their open-mouthed staring into space to the real task in hand: why are the men of Galilee looking into the clouds when there is work to be done beyond the confines of the immediate neighbourhood?

There is a real grace, both required and shown, in moving on in life. We truly need help to leave a place we have known and loved and in which we have been known and loved. The

Ascension invites us to adopt the perspective both of the one departing and of those watching the departure: being either side of an airport departure gate is a familiar enough one for most people. The temptation is to wait until the last possible moment, until our loved ones disappear from sight or until we head out of view. Of course departures extend to every sphere of life: the moment comes when we must take a decisive step on our onward journeys or allow others to continue on theirs. Sometimes we need a little shove to get us started.

Pentecost: On the Holy Spirit as teacher

Given their destructive power, the key symbols of the Spirit – wind and flame – are often rendered remarkably tame. The union of these two explosive elements serve to 'fire' the Apostles into the foundation stones of the Church.

In the midst of imparting new knowledge, a fundamental element of education is reminding learners of what they know already. Jesus has 'co-opted' the Spirit into his teaching ministry, promising that the Holy Spirit would remind the apostles of all he had said to them (c.f. John 14:26). Memory is a fluid thing, dependent on many other factors, but the particular role of the Spirit is to ensure that the hearers of Christ's words were re-minded, somehow made present again at the moment when his words first reached them, and enabled to make the jump between 'then' and 'now'.

The Assumption: On promises fulfilled

This mystery takes a leap beyond the accounts of scripture and leaves us in a place where the faith-story of the Church begins to speak and recount God's continuing intervention in our world. It is part of that tradition that Mary lived out the rest of her 'Easter life' in John's house. It is, of course, to John's tradition that we owe the record of that strange event at the wedding feast at Cana, when a mother asked a son to help. At the end of her days Mary fell asleep 'marked with the sign of faith', as one 'who believed that the promise made her by the Lord would be fulfilled' (Luke 1:45).

The Assumption offers the 'sacramental corollary' to Cana: 'doing whatever he tells you' flowers into the remarkable revelation of a God who does whatever he tells us. In a world tainted with cynicism, we tend to despair of anything being quite as it seems or purports to be. Having made that step of faith in embracing the message of the Assumption, we are asked to mirror that same faith ourselves, in honouring our promises to others – to the 'greatest' and the 'least'.

The Coronation of the Blessed Virgin amid the Rejoicing of the Saints: On sharing the joy of others

In the last mystery of the Rosary, which surpasses all others in scope, we are finally invited to contemplate an 'event' in which we might participate at first-hand. In Mary crowned Queen of Heaven we have a gesture which transcends time and challenges the temptation to saccharine scepticism. Anything which is predicated of the Blessed Virgin is, by extension, applied to us. The crowning of the girl who features in the very first mystery of the Rosary is in fact an endorsement of our whole mixed-up race. We should all rejoice in being so highly favoured since the woman who stands at the end of our race is, quite emphatically, intervening in our lives for the good.

The Communion of Saints is a somewhat whispered presence in the Rosary and yet it is fitting that this great prayer should dovetail neatly with the closing line of the Creed. Every time this statement of faith is professed, we subscribe to a belief that, beyond our sight, there is a vast company of people who care about us. In a passionate negation of the anti-creed which claims that nothing matters, such articles of faith draw our attention to a basic Christian attitude which sees the blessedness of others as intrinsically bound up with our own. On the ground, this mystery invites us to share wholeheartedly in the joys and successes of others. When petty, sin-tainted envies encroach, we should in fact rejoice in the fact that we are all being 'built-up' by the victories of God's love at work. By the same token, our achievements reflect upon others: we are all enriched in the economy of Grace. Here and now, however, how graciously do we deal with praise and commendation heaped upon a colleague?

BLESSINGS AND REFLECTIONS FOR TEACHERS

The texts set out below are ways of celebrating teaching as a profession and a vocation. They may be incorporated into a Eucharistic liturgy or a service of recollection. Like all examples, they can be modified to suit the particular circumstances of the group or occasion.

PRAYER OF COMMISSIONING FOR THE MINISTRY OF TEACHING

Be signed + with the Cross of Salvation
and carry with you the Light of Christ.
May you be strengthened for the ministry
of educating the young
by the love and prayers of this community.

May the Blessing which you have received
and the graces you take with you
reflect upon all whose lives you touch,
especially in your teaching
and guiding of young people.

May the memory of this gathering
and the support of our prayers
continue to strengthen you
in the months and years which lie ahead
and in every situation
to which your vocation will lead you.

We ask all this
through Christ our Lord,
our Teacher and our Brother.

Amen.

A Blessing for New Teachers

God, our Father,
source of wisdom and truth,
we ask your blessing on these new teachers.

May they never forget the dignity
and the challenge of that title: teacher.
It was given to your Son,
who came to teach us
how to be fully alive.
Help them to learn, as he taught,
that 'teacher' is also 'servant'.

And so, my friends,
May you find joy in teaching those
eager to learn.
May you find grace in loving
the unloved.
May you find life at the end of your journey.

And may the peace and blessing of
Almighty God
+ the Father, the Son and the Holy Spirit
come down upon you and
remain with you forever.

Amen.

DEUS CARITAS EST

God is love:

Lord Jesus, help us to grasp that great truth
and to translate it into action.

God is love:

It is by loving that we truly become God's
children.
It is by loving that we discover God's image
within us.
It is by loving that we respond to the invitation
you write on our hearts.

God is love:

May we see all things through the eyes of love.
May those entrusted to our care come to see
themselves as you see them.
May we see our world, scarred and wounded as
it is, as a world redeemed and healed by you.

God is love:

In a world of competing loves, may we never
be afraid to propose you, Lord, as the key
which unlocks the mystery of our nature.
In a world of such hunger, may we offer you as
the nourishment which alone can satisfy.